THE WORDZ WE WEAR

HOW TO **SHOW UP** WITH
CONFIDENCE
AND CREATE **YOUR BEST LIFE**

The Wordz We Wear
2023 YGTMedia Co. Press Trade Paperback Edition
Copyright © 2023 Vera Milan Gervais

Photographer: Darius Bashar
Illustrator: Made Wirawan
Editor: Christine Stock
Book Designer: Michelle Fairbanks

All Rights Reserved. No part of this book can be scanned, distributed, or copied without permission. This book or any portion thereof may not be reproduced or used in any manner whatsoever without the express written permission of the publisher at publishing@ygtmedia.co—except for the use of brief quotations in a book review.

The author has made every effort to ensure the accuracy of the information within this book was correct at time of publication. The author does not assume and hereby disclaims any liability to any party for any loss, damage, or disruption caused by errors or omissions, whether such errors or omissions result from accident, negligence, or any other cause.

The publisher is not responsible for websites (or their content) that are not owned by the publisher.

Published in Canada, for Global Distribution by YGTMedia Co.

www.ygtmedia.co

For more information email: publishing@ygtmedia.co

ISBN trade paperback: 978-1-998754-44-1

eBook: 978-1-998754-45-8

To order additional copies of this book:
publishing@ygtmedia.co

VERA MILAN GERVAIS

THE WORDZ WE WEAR

HOW TO **SHOW UP** WITH **CONFIDENCE** AND CREATE **YOUR BEST LIFE**

To the love of my life, Marcel Anthony Gervais:
you believed in me before I believed in myself.
To Danai and Kyle: you taught me love is unlimited
and life is an endless adventure of discovery.

Dedication

INTRODUCTION 01
- Don't put a ceiling on yourself 07
- About this book 11
- The theory behind Wordz We Wear® 15
- It's your journey 19

PART 1: HOW DID WE BECOME WHO WE ARE? 21
1. We are who we think we are 29
2. We are who we need to be to fit in 41
3. We live up to our labels and nicknames 51
4. We become who we expect to be 59

PART 2: WHY DO WE HOLD OURSELVES BACK? 65
5. Being good prevents us from being great 71
6. Fitting in prevents us from being ourselves 79
7. Being good is never good enough, and perfection is impossible ... 87
8. Wanting more is seen as selfish 97

PART 3: HOW DO WE FIND OURSELVES? 109
9. Trauma and trouble force us out of our comfort zones 117
10. Mentors, muses, and mothers model possibilities 127
11. Identity becomes a journey 141
12. Intentional choices shape our future 151

PART 4: WHAT DOES SUCCESS LOOK LIKE? 161
13. Success is an emotion 167
14. Success is believing 177
15. Success is an identity 185
16. Wordz of Wisdom 195

THE LAST WORDZ 213
Wordz of Gratitude 219
End Notes 224
The Wordz We Wear Book Club Prompts 225
Author Bio 227

INTRODUCTION

I wasn't a normal kid. By the time I was eight years old, my left leg was four inches shorter than my right, and my left foot was two sizes smaller.

I had been born defective.

I suspect my parents were never told the extent of what was wrong with my body. I'm not even sure the doctors knew. Since I was born near the end of the polio epidemic, it was easy to assume my birth defect was a result of exposure to polio.

The truth is a little more complicated. I have Proximal Femoral Focal Deficiency (PFFD), which means that one of the bones in my thigh, the femur, didn't grow properly. Neither did my kneecap, nor my ankle. As a result, my lower leg rotated outward and my knee wasn't stable.

I was visibly different from other kids, and kids say it like it is. Just months after I'd started school, my mismatched legs had defined me. I was "The Crippled Girl."

The label stuck because it described the girl they saw. The four surgeries I had between the ages of eight and seventeen meant I missed months of school and returned in a wheelchair or on crutches. Even when those hated accessories went into a closet until the next time, I didn't fit in.

I couldn't do what other kids did. I was unable to participate in normal childhood activities like running and jumping. When I tried, I lost my balance and fell. Neighbors and classmates quickly learned to stay away from me so that they wouldn't be accused of knocking me over. Besides, they didn't want to *catch* whatever it was that caused my strange legs. Given that polio is highly contagious, it wasn't an unrealistic phobia.

My life was defined by limits.

Those limits weren't just because my leg didn't grow properly. I grew up with seven sisters—no brothers. We were close in age, with only ten years separating the eldest from the youngest.

Mom and Dad managed their gaggle of girls with discipline. We had strict rules regarding acceptable behavior. In retrospect, I understand our parents' intent was to protect us, but it wasn't explained that way. Rules were rules. Period. Mom and Dad focused on maintaining harmony and avoiding any potential for conflict.

Don't interrupt when adults are speaking.
Teachers are always right; don't correct them.
Girls don't play rough sports.
Get good grades.
Get better grades.

There were a lot of *don'ts* in our lives, which often left us tiptoeing with a sense of uncertainty, wondering if we could do anything right. We were expected to be quiet and obedient, to listen to our parents and teachers, to get along with each other, and to obey the Church.

It's no wonder many of my childhood memories are about hiding. I hid from the bullies who found me an easy target, and I hid to avoid the stares and comments of strangers who pointed and whispered. I also hid my curiosity, so I wouldn't break the rules. In essence, I hid from life.

I felt safe when I was part of the backdrop—when I was invisible. I learned to avoid attention by becoming a chameleon, following the rules, and staying out of the limelight. I did my physical therapy, got good grades, and coped with pain by escaping into books.

But being invisible meant I also hid my gifts, my strengths, and my dreams. I didn't feel they mattered.

I'm not the only one who hid my best self.

So many people, particularly women and marginalized individuals, bury the best parts of themselves because their talents and attributes make them stand out—and standing out is not always acceptable.

Too many of us are taught that being inquisitive and speaking up are not appropriate behaviors. We're brought up under the cloud of *Being Good*. We're told we must *Behave. Be quiet. Look after everyone else.* It's our role. It's expected.

The problem with doing what's expected—doing what we're told—is that we unconsciously limit ourselves. We get stuck in patterns that don't allow us to express the passions and talents at the core of who we are. We focus on helping others grow and thrive, and we miss out on our own development and happiness. We play small.

When we play small, we stay small.

We rationalize our choices by telling ourselves we're being responsible. Maybe we are. But the flip side of meeting other people's expectations of who we *should* be, is that we limit who we *could* be. So why do we allow ourselves to be defined and confined?

Who planted the seeds of doubt that grow with abandon in our minds? Who set the rules and boundaries that restrict our choices? And who permitted these artificial constraints to procreate and become the common law of acceptable behavior . . . the unwritten laws casting judgment on us?

I may not have a degree in psychology, but I am a writer. I've spent decades writing health and wellness information as well as advertising and marketing materials. I know how words can persuade and influence, leading to both positive and negative outcomes. I understand the power of words on our mindsets, and the power of images on our actions.

And I know how our expectations directly impact who we become and what we achieve.

DON'T PUT A CEILING ON YOURSELF

Every time you state what you want or believe, you're the first to hear it. It's a message to both you and others about what you think is possible. Don't put a ceiling on yourself. —Oprah Winfrey

---

We know about the Glass Cciling, the invisible ceiling standing between us and our dreams and goals. We didn't ask for this barrier, but it still holds us back.

What about the other ceilings that stop us from achieving our full potential? The ceilings we unwittingly allow to limit us when we accept labels and expectations of success or failure based on the thoughts and opinions of others?

The messages we receive growing up are powerful predictors of our lives. Positive messaging sets us up to expect it's possible to follow our hearts, believe in our dreams, and create possibilities:

You can do anything if you set your mind to it.

You can be whoever you want to be.

Don't let others tell you what to do.

There's nothing stopping you except you.

Then there are the belittling and shaming warnings so many of us hear. Rather than empowering us to live fully, they crush our dreams and motivation:

You can't make a living doing that.

You'll never succeed.

Make me proud.

Your father/grandfather would be so disappointed in you.

Don't ruin the family reputation.

What makes you think you deserve that?

Who would hire you for that?

How can you do this to me?

Don't get too big for your britches.

These messages get ingrained in our psyches. They send signals to our brains that can either set us up with the confidence to succeed or sabotage our ability to live fully.

It's time to challenge the beliefs that create invisible ceilings and give ourselves permission to be who we want to be. It's time to expect more—and get more—out of life. We can, by intentionally creating our own expectations of what we can and can't do, and what we do and don't deserve.

My journey to unraveling this complex knot of expectations that society places on people, and particularly on women, comes from my own struggle with identity.

When we accept it's okay to want more, we give ourselves permission to go for more, to break through the Glass Ceiling, the Identity Ceiling™, the Education Ceiling™, and the Expectations Ceiling™ to achieve our dreams.

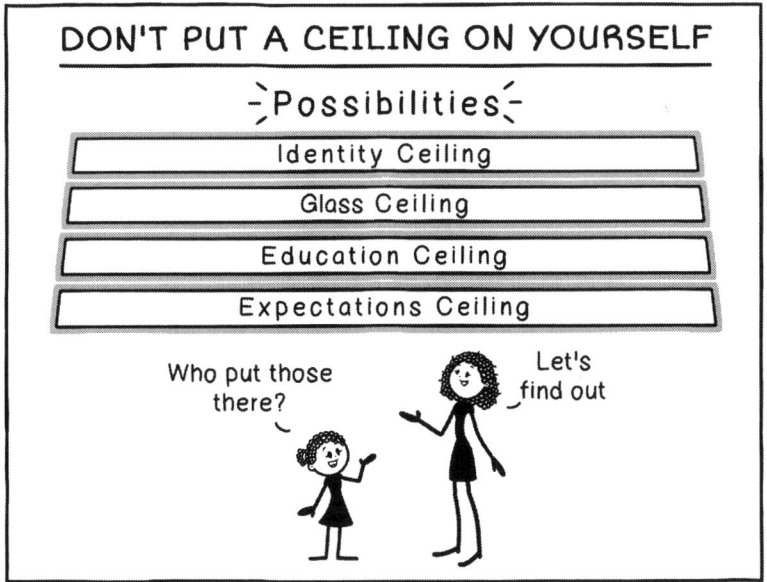

ABOUT THIS BOOK

This book focuses on women because I believe it's time for women to own their identity. At the same time, the impact of words and expectations on who we become affects everyone. We can all benefit from knowing how to use language to step into our power and embrace unlimited possibilities.

I am honored to be able to touch on the struggles and successes of almost thirty women on these pages: businesswomen, entrepreneurs, artists, professionals, politicians, wives, mothers, coaches, colleagues, introverts, and fiercely independent women who have given themselves the time, space, and permission to abandon guilt and step into being all they can be.

I first shared my thoughts and theories with friends and family, then reached out to women I met in masterminds and at conferences as well as through my company, my community, and my connections. I asked them about their dreams and doubts, their expectations, and challenges. I asked how they embraced their passions, made decisions, overcame reluctance and resistance, and created the lives they wanted to live.

The stories and struggles these women shared are different from each other, but they prove that women can and do change the world. Their experiences and perspectives show what our lives can be like when we choose to live our best life—however we define it.

The sad fact is that most of us are not taught to believe—or even admit—that it's okay to want to do more and be more. Yet we do! We often ache to express some integral part of ourselves, whether it's our creativity, compassion, excitement, intelligence, or an urge to save the world. That ache to express ourselves is a common thread weaving through the stories women related to me. It's an ache often repressed because of external pressures.

Take jewelry designer Anne-Marie Warburton. As a young girl, she fantasized about being on a talk show. She imagined herself engaged in animated conversation, knowing that people listened to her because her opinion mattered. But no one encouraged this vibrant young woman to stand up and speak. In fact, people constantly told her to be quiet because her zest for life and learning was overwhelming.

Discouraged, Anne-Marie silenced her voice and did what was expected of her. She married young and supported her husband while he pursued an education. Instead of speaking up, she slid into the background. She summarized that phase of her life by saying, "As a young married woman, I didn't think I had any importance at all."

Veronica Piacek, on the other hand, had a supportive family environment. Yet she inadvertently created her own barriers through a sense of duty. As the youngest, she was her immigrant mother's last hope to have a doctor in the family. Since Veronica didn't want to disappoint her mother, she felt obliged to study health sciences instead of exploring her creative side.

The pressure to comply to other people's expectations can be direct, as it was with Anne-Marie, or subtle and unintentional, like Veronica experienced. Either way, it affects our expectations of what we can or should do.

There is no single answer to how we become our best selves. The goal is to move toward living with purpose, because having purpose allows us to acknowledge we matter . . . to accept that we have choices, and to give ourselves permission to follow our hearts and our dreams.

We can't begin to fully embrace the possibilities in our lives until we understand why we are who we are, and what's holding us back from living fully.

I no longer believe my life is insignificant. I am healthy and active and have been happily married for more than three decades. I have two incredible, independent adult children and some affectionate grand-dogs. My sense of adventure has taken me to all seven continents with my family.

I've been an accountant, analyst, advertising agency executive, copywriter, entrepreneur, and strategic consultant. Leaving those identities behind helped me evolve into my current identities as an author, keynote speaker, mindset mentor, workshop facilitator, and award-winning businesswoman—and there's still more I want to become!

The good news is that no matter how long we've been hiding in the shadows, we can always step into brighter futures. We can change the limiting scripts looping around in our heads and explore a limitless range of possibilities. We can own our identity.

THE THEORY BEHIND WORDZ WE WEAR®

We live in a world where *Identity* needs to be defined. We need to know *Who we are* so we can become *Who we want to be*. That needs *words*. Without words, how do we describe ourselves? How would people know who we are, what we do, why we care, and how we show up?

Words provide a frame of reference to figure out where we belong in the world. As a result, the words we use when we talk about ourselves have a huge impact on what we believe about ourselves, as well as what other people think about us.

The big question is—do we stop to think about those words? The word labels we use to describe ourselves are like clothing labels. They have an impact on how we feel and how we show up in the world. But *words* themselves are generic. They create nice, neat little boxes we can fit ourselves into . . . assuming we want to fit into boxes with everyone else.

""Wordz," spelled with a zed (or zee), as it is in the title of this book, disrupt conditioned thought patterns. The unexpected spelling causes us to pause. To stop and think. We can create the same pattern disruption when we consciously choose the wordz we use to talk about ourselves.

Intentionally embracing the psychological power of word labels changes the way we think and feel about ourselves. We can consciously cultivate our wordz and thoughts to gain confidence and transform how we show up.

In essence, the Wordz We Wear create an image of who we are:

- Δ   Our self-image influences the way we feel about ourselves.
- Δ   The way we feel about ourselves shapes the way we show up.
- Δ   The way we show up affects perceptions of who we are and what we can do.
- Δ   When we show up with confidence, we expect more.
- Δ   When we expect more, we pursue more.
- Δ   When we pursue more, we get more.
- Δ   We grow. We own our identity.

IT'S YOUR JOURNEY

This book is structured in four parts, because we are all at different places on our journeys.

PART 1: How did we become who we are?

PART 2: Why do we hold ourselves back?

PART 3: How do we find ourselves?

PART 4: What does success look like?

I invite you to begin wherever you want to. Read cover to cover or jump around. It doesn't matter. What matters is that when you leave the page, you will know beyond a doubt that you are more than enough. You will believe that you deserve more than mediocre—you can choose an unlimited life. You can be who you choose to become.

Are you ready to resist the ceilings that limit you, and own your wordz, your choices, your identity, and your future?

Let's begin.

PART 1:

How did we become who we are?

> WHAT I DO ISN'T WHO I AM, AND WHO I AM ISN'T WHAT I DO.
> WE NEED TO SEPARATE THE TWO. –RENÉE WARREN

Not the reception I expected.

I sat at my desk, tears dripping on the stack of invoices trembling in my hands. It hadn't even been two weeks. I'd lost everything in less than two weeks.

When I joined an oil and gas company in the '70s, I was the only female accountant in the office. I was young and idealistic and saw my hiring as a huge win for women. I thought I'd be congratulated for breaking a barrier.

Boy, did I have a lot to learn.

The office manager gave me documents to sign and guided me through a round of introductions. Finishing in the kitchen, she pointed to a schedule. My name appeared all five days the following week.

It was the coffee and reception-relief rotation. I didn't drink coffee, and I'd never been trained on handling reception duties. I was confused. I scanned the list. None of the other accountants were on it.

Apparently, I wasn't an accountant for this agenda. I was female. My skills and training didn't matter. My gender established my place in the world of kitchen duty—a stereotype enforced by the women in the office. What was I supposed to say? I didn't want to alienate anyone on my first day.

Monday morning started with a chorus of complaints about the coffee. It wasn't like I'd tried to make it taste bad. I didn't know how much coffee to add to the carafe, so the first batch was a tepid tea color. The second one could have tarred a driveway. The office manager glared accusingly at me as she grabbed a red marker and wrote detailed instructions for me to follow the next day.

But the best was to come on Wednesday.

The company had a phone system that was old-fashioned, even for the '70s. Think of old movies where the operator is connected to a switchboard with a headset. The board itself was a jumble of cords hanging from numbered slots. The cords had to be moved around to allow callers to reach various extensions . . . I guess that's why it was called a switchboard.

Wednesday was someone's birthday and the women were going for a girls' lunch to celebrate, leaving me, a twenty-year-old accountant, to handle reception. Apparently, five minutes of training made me an expert.

As the women were putting on their coats, one of them mentioned that the president was expecting a call from the board of directors. Then they walked out the door.

On cue, the phone rang. The board was calling for Mr. W.

"Certainly, let me patch you through."

Open the line . . . tell Mr. W. the call was connecting . . . tell the board I was connecting them to Mr. W. . . . plug the cords in . . . done.

Oops, I could hear people talking. I'd forgotten to disconnect myself. Unplug.

A lot of cursing preceded the president as he came charging down the hall. I hadn't disconnected myself; I had unplugged the board of directors.

I cringed under his tirade and promised to not mess up again.

The phone rang. The board was calling—again.

"Certainly, I'm sorry I cut you off. Let me patch you through."

Carefully now: Open the line . . . tell Mr. W. the call was coming through . . . tell the board I was connecting them . . . plug the cords in . . . check the lines . . . disconnect myself . . . done.

With a long exhale, I pushed back from the desk . . . catching the arm of my chair on a cord.

Mr. W. came screaming down the hall again, just as one of the women returned to get a forgotten birthday gift. Pointing at her, he yelled, "Get me the board of directors, immediately. And you," he said, turning to me, "You're fired. I never want to see you on the switchboard again."

I ran back to my desk shaking, knowing the entire office would learn how angry I'd made the president. Crying, too embarrassed to leave the shelter of my cubby, I picked up a pile of invoices and started entering them in a spreadsheet.

Hours later the office manager came to an abrupt stop beside me.

"What are you doing here?"

"My job."

"I thought Mr. W. fired you."

I stared at the spreadsheet I'd just completed, angry at the injustice. I was a crappy receptionist, but I was a good accountant. That's what I'd been hired for. Whether they had intended to or not, the other women in the company had set me up to fail. They'd succeeded in crushing my dreams in under two weeks.

Except . . . except, damn it . . . I looked at the work I'd done and knew the report was in better shape than it had been before I was hired. If I was going to be judged, I wanted it to be for the right reasons.

I sat up straight and looked this woman in the eyes.

"He fired me from reception, not from the accounting department."

I might have made enemies of some of the women that day, but I also made life easier for the next female accountant.

She wasn't put on the coffee rotation schedule.

1. WE ARE WHO WE THINK WE ARE.

*We can't define ourselves solely by what we do;
we need to know who we are.* –Dawn Arnold

Who do you see when you look at yourself? Do you see a beautiful soul full of energy and possibilities? Or do you see the lines and wrinkles of worry you've earned from looking after others?

Do you see the love in your eyes and the strength in your shoulders? Or do you see the physical weight of unlived dreams and heavy responsibilities?

When you look in a mirror, do you see the wonderful being you are, or do you see someone you don't want to be?

Mirrors supposedly reflect our images back at us, yet they can distort our images. Some clothing store mirrors make us look taller and slimmer (thank you), while fun-house mirrors completely rearrange our features. Neither gives us accurate reflections of ourselves. Yet we look into mirrors as if they can show us who we are.

They can't. Mirrors reflect an image distorted by what our friends, families, and strangers project onto us.

We see who we expect to see.

When we hear what others say about who we are, who they think we should be, or who they want us to be, we question ourselves. It's instinctive. We care what people think, and our instinctive need to be accepted allows other people to influence our sense of worthiness.

We even allow strangers to judge us and define who we are.

In today's digitally connected environment, cultivating an image we can proudly—or at least safely—project to the world is almost compulsory. On top of juggling everything else on our to-do lists, we need to worry about how people we don't even know see and judge both our physical attributes and our lives.

Are we attractive enough? Active enough? Have we achieved enough?

Whether we're running businesses or households or pursuing education or careers, we may find ourselves expected to take care of everyone around us, while still making time to be fit, friendly, and fulfilled.

Did I miss anything on that list?

Social media, social norms, and social pressures have created the expectation that we must *do it all*—and do it well. Personal branding is big business, even for people who don't have a business. Ironically, even being *authentic* has morphed into a strategic goal. It's become part of an intentionally designed image of who we are . . . but too often it projects an image we think others are looking for.

No wonder we question ourselves!

When we look into mirrors, we see what we expect to see. When we're tired, we focus on the lines around our lips and the circles under our eyes. When we're excited, we see the sparkle in our eyes and the color in our cheeks. When we're happy, we like who we see in the mirror. When we're stressed or overwhelmed, we find all the flaws that prove we're not good enough.

What we see is amplified by the voices in our heads—voices reassuring us we're doing our best, or voices replaying all the negativity we've heard in the past. Whether we listen to the Cheerleaders or the Nags, the messages we hear start to sound like truths, because we've heard them over and over.

We may think our brains are rational, but they're not. Our brains don't actually know the difference between truth and fiction. They simply look for patterns, interpret them, and accept repetition as reality.

That's the scary part. Familiarity creates beliefs that are false truths. We hang on to those beliefs and biases because we have been exposed to them from the moment we were born. We believe them.

What our thoughts conceive, the brain believes. That's what mindset is—imprinted beliefs dictating how we think and influencing our choices and actions. Not surprisingly, our actions align with the beliefs embedded in our minds, so our behaviors reflect those beliefs. Perception becomes reality.

What we think affects our choices. If we believe one of our roles is to ensure everyone is safe and happy, a sense of obligation rests with us every day. If we believe we can never meet the standards others have set, we may feel defeated even before we start.

Thoughts are powerful. They're the filter through which we see the options and choices available to us. Thoughts create and shape our expectations of what we can or can't do and do or don't deserve.

Unfortunately, thoughts based on external expectations often crush our dreams.

As a child, Alicia Grayeb was always dreaming. She dreamt of being an astronaut or maybe an astronomer. She dreamt of being able to change the things she felt weren't fair. And she dreamt of ways to save the planet. But life didn't quite align with those dreams. While her parents supported her when she talked about her ideas and ambitions, her Mexican culture wasn't as conducive to this thirst for learning and change. The contradiction confused the young girl. Her mom told her she could be anything she wanted to be, but the environment in which she lived was steeped in tradition and resistant to change. Alicia felt out of place in her own community.

By the time she was eighteen, Alicia had to make peace with reinventing herself. Even as a teenager, her sense of self was strong enough that she knew her future would be decided by the culture she was living in. She realized she had to break away from traditions that didn't serve her. In her mind, that meant she had to fly or die. Alicia took control of her identity the only way she knew she could—by changing her environment. She left Mexico when she was twenty.

We become who we think we can be.

The power of expectations on our unconscious minds is as insidious as it is invisible. Expectations create thought patterns that form endless loops in our subconscious, reinforcing our beliefs, whether they are empowering or limiting. Ironically, the beliefs that affect our expectations about our future come from what we've been conditioned to think in the past. We carry forward these beliefs, often without realizing how they influence our choices.

When we understand our belief systems, our choices may be clearer.

Dawn Arnold was a born leader who innately knew people need direction. She expected to change the game. She eagerly stepped into roles where she could organize things, from Student Council to the

Frye Festival, Canada's only international bilingual literary festival. Rather than wait for life to happen, she focused on making connections, sharing ideas, and seeing the larger picture.

Dawn had the confidence to take on these challenges because her parents told her she could do anything—*as long as she didn't screw up*. While this perfectionist script may have caused some of us to hold back, it inspired Dawn. The caveat not to mess up made her consciously think about how she could successfully push boundaries and do things differently. She pressed on, expecting she would face challenges. And she did. People challenged her ambition, her vision, her opinions, and the way she stood up for her values. Dawn managed to stay focused by adopting the attitude that challenges are part of the journey; they're steps along the way.

Dawn's journey led her to politics. She ran for City Council and then mayor of Moncton, New Brunswick, Canada. She became the city's first female mayor, and she was re-elected to her second term with 58 percent of the vote, despite some nastiness directed at her during the campaign. In many ways, the advice Dawn's parents gave her served her well. She expected to be scrutinized as a woman in a leadership position, so she accepted the inevitable, determined to show up and become a role model for other women.

We are who we think we are and who we say we are. We become

who we believe we can become. Which means we are who we expect we should be and become who we expect to become.

But what is at the root of those expectations? Who and what shapes them? What raises them? Who crushes them? What factors create the ceilings that hold us back from doing more, being more, and becoming more?

Some people blame the Glass Ceiling, an intangible barrier preventing many women and minorities from advancing in their careers and businesses. However, the barriers preventing women and minorities from advancing extend beyond the realm of career and business, beyond cultural conditioning, and beyond geographic and economic boundaries. These struggles reflect systemic beliefs and biases around what individuals deserve.

Beliefs and biases are learned. Many women are taught one of their key responsibilities is to take on caregiver roles. Family obligations add another layer of expectations. Religion and culture may also impose constraints. Then human nature adds the desire to be liked. There's more than one layer to the ceilings holding us back from living fully.

Our beliefs and biases influence our actions and choices. If we don't believe we can accomplish or achieve something—and if others don't believe in us and support us—those real and perceived boundaries hold us back from trying. If we don't try, nothing changes.

On the other hand, our beliefs can empower us. If we believe we are meant to create something or do something with our innate talents and gifts, that mindset can fuel our commitment and our choices.

Julia Sen, the Possibility Psychologist, falls into the second category. Julia viewed the Glass Ceiling as a mindset she had the ability to step through. "I didn't see myself held to the traditional limits of a South Asian woman. I felt like I had options." Because she didn't see a ceiling on possibilities, it didn't exist for her.

If we can break through the Glass Ceiling by ignoring it, maybe it's more fragile than we think.

Alex Cattoni, founder of the Copy Posse, didn't grow up thinking she was limited because she was a girl. She had watched her mother build an incredible career and raise a family despite the challenges she faced, so Alex didn't believe being female should stand in the way of her becoming who she wanted to be. Alex credits her mother with teaching her that even though life can be tough, if she is tough too, she can do whatever she wants. These beliefs ultimately led Alex to launch a business that gives her the flexibility and freedom she wants, while helping others use their voices to create the lives and businesses they've always dreamed of.

Sometimes the motivation to achieve comes from defying others' opinions. Melissa Duguay started telling her parents at a very young age that she wanted to be a hairdresser. It was the only thing she ever wanted to do. She believed she'd been born to become a stylist. Imagine her surprise when the high school counselor told her she should be more practical and become a secretary. Why? Because she would never make enough money in hairdressing! The counselor was crushing Melissa's dreams without exploring why they mattered to the young girl.

"At that moment I knew I had something to prove. As I walked out of her office, I turned and promised her I would make more money than she did." Gaining experience and building her clientele took a few years, but Melissa persisted and fulfilled her promise to that counselor. She now has numerous prestigious Contessa and Mirror awards and a reputation as one of the world's leading platform hairstyle artists. Melissa expected she could become who she wanted to be, and she did.

These women believed in themselves. They didn't accept limits; they set their own expectations. They knew what they wanted to achieve, and they set out to find a way. They owned their identities.

Our expectations shape our identity.

The expectations set by our parents, peers, preachers, and teachers foster our beliefs about who we are and what possibilities exist in our futures. Sometimes those expectations align with our individual goals and values, and we feel supported in our growth. Other times beliefs collide, and the pressure of others' expectations can suppress our hopes and dreams.

Whatever our expectations are, they shape us. We fall to the level of low expectations and rise to meet higher expectations.

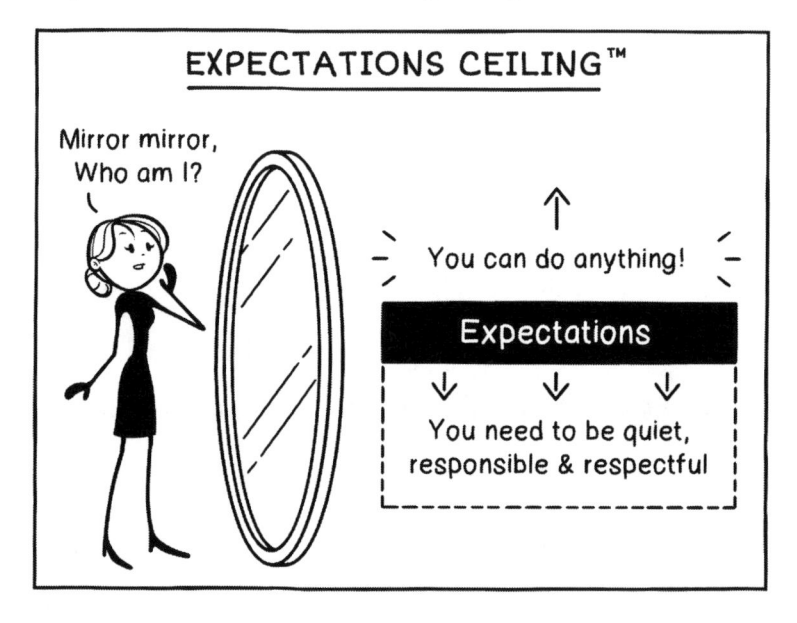

EXPECTATIONS CEILING™

Mirror mirror, Who am I?

You can do anything!

Expectations

You need to be quiet, responsible & respectful

Psychologists call the influence of expectations the Pygmalion Effect.[1] This effect was dramatically demonstrated in a study where teachers were told which of their students were gifted. When the academic results were later analyzed, those "gifted" students did indeed perform better. The catch was, the students weren't all gifted.

Gifted was only a label; it did not reflect the students' innate intelligence and capabilities. Yet when they were treated as gifted and supported by their teachers, all the students stepped up and reached new levels. That's how much people's expectations shape what we do.

Expectations affect who we become. We accept the advantages or limits that we believe we deserve, and we become who we believe we should be.

Our growth stops at the Expectations Ceiling.

Maybe it's not a Glass Ceiling that holds us back. The Expectations Ceiling sets limits on who we are taught to be and who we believe we can become. Our choices and actions will reflect who we expect to be.

Whether our expectations are high or low, the reality is we spend our life living up to them or down from them. If we are living according to other people's expectations of who we are and what we deserve—if we don't own our expectations—we don't own our identity. We don't become fully expressed. We become shadows of our true selves.

A pause for thought before we leave this chapter:

Here's why we are who we think we are:

We see who we expect to see.
We become who we think we can be.
Our expectations shape our identity.
Our growth stops at the Expectations Ceiling.

2. WE ARE WHO WE NEED TO BE TO FIT IN.

When we don't feel included, we don't feel relevant.
–Edye Hoffmann

What do we say when someone asks us who we are? Chances are, we give our name, our relationship to others, or what we do. And chances are, we hesitate when we're asked.

You'd think we'd be prepared for this question and have ready answers, but it isn't that easy. Specific situations or individuals can alter how we feel in the moment, and those feelings dictate our responses to the question.

When I asked women how they describe themselves in social situations, most said they give their name and information relevant to the moment:

I'm Mary's sister.

I'm Jim's wife.

I'm your new neighbor.

I'm with XYZ corporation.

Why do we hold back from expressing who we are at our core? Why don't women—for that matter, why don't most people—introduce what makes them unique?

I'm an obsessive reader.

I knit clothing for the homeless.

I'm a rare-orchid gardener.

I'm a sustainability-focused interior designer.

I'm an anti-ageism advocate.

Why do we resist standing out? Because we have an innate need to fit in.

Fitting in creates safety and connection.

The way we introduce ourselves places us into certain groups or communities. It allows people to position us within frameworks they understand, creating a sense of comfort and connection. In other words, we adapt the way we describe ourselves so we can relate to others and help them accept us.

Reformed perfectionist Stephanie Major knows the art of this delicate dance well. She knows a part of her is a people pleaser who wants to make everyone happy, and that can affect how she shows up.

"I learned how to conform to the group opinion. One of my tactics was to be quiet so I wasn't really agreeing with everyone, but I wasn't disagreeing either. I was remaining neutral. I was respectful and nice so they liked having me around and let me be a part of things."

Stephanie leaned into a role as an organizer and facilitator, which allowed her to learn and network. Staying neutral exposed her to many visionaries and influencers, but it didn't give Stephanie the opportunity to explore her own points of view and opinions. Being a sponge filled her with knowledge but left her unfulfilled.

Establishing relationships that recognize our individuality is more fulfilling. According to Edye Hoffmann, the way we are known creates memorability. Edye is passionate about creating support networks that allow individuals with dementia to remain involved in community and life. Within those community and social circles, she's known as the "Dementia Lady," but Edye prefers the way people with dementia have described her: the American lady with the big teeth.

"Many people don't know how to pronounce my name, but people with dementia won't necessarily remember my name anyway. They will still want to describe the person they have a relationship with, and I think the biggest compliment is to be remembered for a big smile, warm hospitality, my accent, or the stories around how I arrived in Britain." Those attributes identify Edye. They create connection.

Identifying ourselves by our relationships is not only an easy response, but it also communicates an important part of who we are. Many married women are accustomed to being identified as their spouse's wife or partner. Some women are okay with this title but others feel they lose their identity, especially when their spouses are successful or famous individuals. These reactions are subjective and formed by their individual perspectives.

Catherine is okay with being identified as "the speaker's wife" because she chose her role as facilitator. "I'm a supporter by nature. I do it well. I don't want to be center stage. That's where my husband shines." Catherine's role as a participating partner in her husband's achievements is important to her. She helped create his success, and she owns her role when she introduces herself as his partner. It's an intentional aspect of her identity.

Work and relationships ground us.

Dawn Arnold readily introduces herself as the mayor of Moncton, a role she's held for years. Without context, though, *mayor* is simply a title. It establishes what Dawn does, not the changes she has made and the impact she's had. The title didn't create her achievements; her courage and determination did. Her accomplishments as mayor are what matters to Dawn. She's intensely proud of her role in bringing progress to the Atlantic Canadian city, making it one of the top ten fastest growing cities in Canada. But there are more sides to Dawn's identity. She's a wife and mother who loves books, and an avid cyclist who routinely rides her bicycle to and from city hall.

Identity has more than one aspect, and our titles form part of it. In a business situation, people tend to say what they do: *I am an accountant, a coach, a writer.* These types of words create both connection and context to establish roles and credibility.

When you think about it, we inherited the tendency to define ourselves by our work. Many surnames reflect the occupations that our forbearers had: Carpenter, Smith, Baker, Miller, Cook. Over time, our occupations ceased to be how we were known, but our names remained part of our identity. They became the labels that placed us within family and community relationships. In essence, they created context for fitting in.

Word labels create a frame of reference that people understand and relate to. Words identify which boxes we fit into, which boxes others fit into, and where the overlap is. Words are how we create connection and feelings of belonging.

Those labels simplify and communicate identity. Maybe we need to rethink simplification, though, because our identity is fluid and complex.

Roles establish identity.

I'm an adventurous introvert, a creative soul, a disruptor, and a dreamer. But no single set of words describes me. In fact, I play with how I introduce myself to others. When I get on an airplane, I change how I identify myself depending on who I'm sitting beside. I always tell the truth, but I pick and choose how I describe who I am.

If my seat partner appears to be a parent or grandparent, I will usually say I'm a mother. I'll brag about my son and daughter, and we'll talk about the joys and challenges of raising kids. Children give us a connection.

On the other hand, if I am sitting beside someone who seems artistic, I will introduce myself as a writer and photographer. I have discovered almost everyone likes to write or take pictures, so those words establish common ground and comfort before we don headsets to watch our movies.

I also have a persona for those smug businesspersons who look down at this small woman who doesn't wear much makeup and peg me as a bland and boring seatmate. I love watching their expressions when I tell them I'm a serial entrepreneur and own commercial property. I am not what they expected me to be.

Why do I do this? Why would I change the way I talk about myself?

To create connection. I might be sitting beside this person for anywhere from two to twelve hours. I don't want to make a lifelong friend, but I do want to be comfortable during my journey. Let's face it, we often describe ourselves certain ways because we believe particular versions of who we are will create connection.

Sally Ng intentionally uses her introduction to connect with who she is talking to, which could be groups of women, students, or potential customers. Sally is an immigrant who has spent a decade navigating her career through the start-up and entrepreneurial world. She is young, outspoken, and successful—and accustomed to people questioning her presence. Sally says they want to know: Is she here because she's a female and a person of color, or does she actually have the expertise?

Sally is an extreme extrovert with high energy. She shows up as a strong woman, so she knows the reception she'll receive depends on her audience's perspectives and expectations. To reduce the potential for intimidating people, she often avoids titles, especially in the inclusion and equity space. At other times, Sally will proudly say she's a pilot, a military officer, a cofounder, a CEO, and a board member. Those roles help her establish her credibility and authority and create trust.

We often identify ourselves by the roles we play. When we use words like mother, wife, partner, sister, friend, writer, or mentor, we're describing our relationships to families, groups, and communities. Those word labels help create a sense of belonging because we feel safe and protected when we are able to relate to others like us. Labels provide a framework for people to identify with us. We fit in the mother, sister, daughter boxes, as do many of the other people around us. Our shared roles allow us to relate to one another, but the expectations attached to those roles can limit our sense of self, especially when we feel the need to be perfect.

Some roles, like being mothers or caregivers for our parents, come with real and perceived obligations. Those *shoulds* affect how we feel, act, and show up to the world.

Stephanie Major, the mother of two young women, says mothers seldom have the option to walk away from their roles. "It would be the lowest of lows for a mother to just be tired or want a break or let someone else take responsibility for a bit. There's a different standard for being a mother than for being a father."

If our communities frown on women working outside the home, on nontraditional relationships, or on creative expression, rising to our greatest potential can be difficult. We stop short when we think we risk belonging.

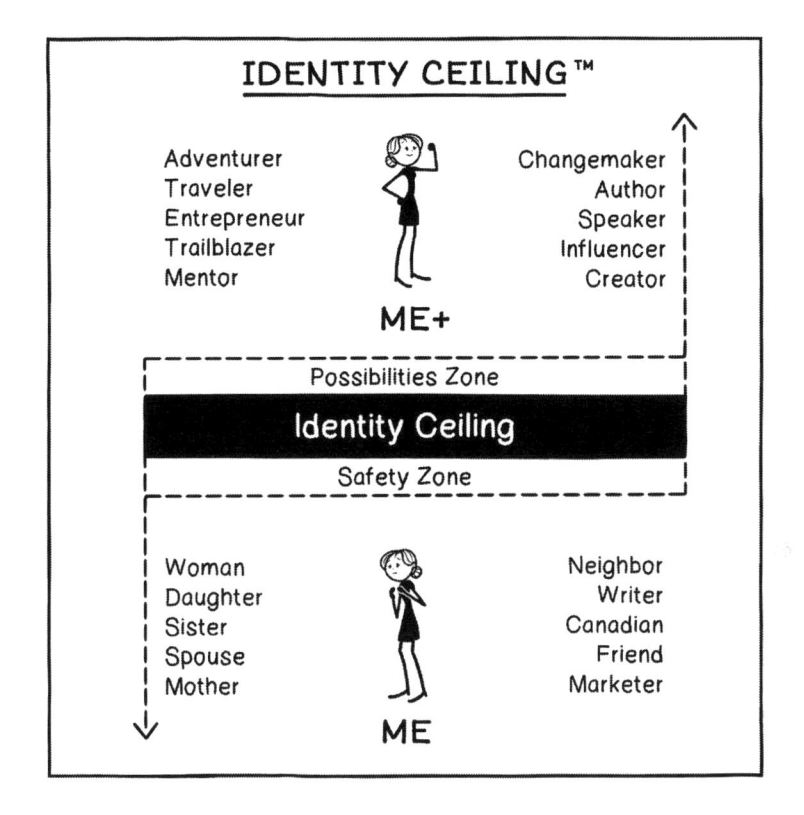

```
                    IDENTITY CEILING™

    Adventurer              Changemaker   ↑
    Traveler                Author        |
    Entrepreneur            Speaker       |
    Trailblazer             Influencer    |
    Mentor                  Creator       |
                   ME+
    - - - - - - - - - - - - - - - - - - -
           Possibilities Zone
           Identity Ceiling
           Safety Zone
    - - - - - - - - - - - - - - - - - - -
    Woman                   Neighbor
    Daughter                Writer
    Sister                  Canadian
    Spouse                  Friend
    Mother                  Marketer
    ↓              ME
```

Fear creates an Identity Ceiling.

The fear of rejection limits our choices and our growth. Our natural instincts to play safe become a ceiling. Not just a Glass Ceiling, an *Identity Ceiling*. A ceiling created by beliefs and expectations about who we are and how we should show up if we want to fit in. To belong. To feel comfortable and safe.

Yet when we're frustrated or anxious or angry at these limits, we may not see how external pressures influence our dissatisfaction. Instead, we blame ourselves for not being more, doing more, and achieving more. Worse yet, we may blame ourselves for not being *enough* because we haven't lived up to expectations others have placed on us.

Even when we push boundaries and pursue the dreams and goals we desire, we question ourselves. Doubt taps on our shoulders, and fear whispers warnings in our ears. We see possibilities, but we feel resistance.

The inner struggle is real. We hit the ceiling on growth and fulfillment when we battle the pressure to behave the way we are expected to. We can't move forward unless we challenge and change those expectations.

If we change our expectations, we change our actions, behaviors, and choices. We own who we are and who we have the potential to become. We own our identity.

A pause for thought before we leave this chapter:

> **Here's why we are
> who we need to be to fit in:**
>
> ---
>
> Fitting in creates safety and connection.
> Work and relationships ground us.
> Roles establish identity.
> Fear creates an Identity Ceiling.

3. WE LIVE UP TO OUR LABELS AND NICKNAMES.

If I didn't define myself for myself, I would be crunched into other people's fantasies for me and eaten alive. –Audre Lorde

---

Our identity begins with a noun announcing our arrival: *It's a boy! It's a girl!*

Then our individuality is christened with a name or names that might honor family heritage, reflect religious significance, pay tribute to a celebrity or trend, or channel a vision. In addition to our formal names, people give us endearments and nicknames. A physical feature or behavior can lead to monikers like Curly, Chubby, or Sleepyhead.

All these names affect the way we are talked to—and talked about—from our earliest moments. They describe us. They label us. They signal how we are seen by others. They define who we believe we are.

Names are labels.

Children want parental approval, so what happens when their nicknames create expectations for how they need to show up?

Think of the nickname Princess. She's your princess now. Does that mean she expects a fairy-tale life? Does she grow up thinking she needs a prince to rescue her? Does she believe she has to be frilly and feminine or you won't love her?

And Slugger. Yep, maybe he or she has a good arm. Maybe your child likes to play ball. But is baseball or tennis or football or swimming a sport your child *wants* to develop, or one they think they *have to* develop because it's important to you?

If your child doesn't make the team, is he, she, or they going to be afraid of disappointing you? Of not living up to what *you* want your child to be? Or even what *you* wanted to be and didn't become?

We use so many terms that set expectations: Sweetheart, Sweet Pea, Angel, Champ, Ace. And if that's not enough to worry about . . . what about the adjectives we use? As parents and teachers, we put children into boxes all the time. Then we add adjectives to differentiate those children from each other: *Good* boy. *Excellent* student. *Quiet* girl.

What we may not realize is that those adjectives are another dimension of labeling that can create its own set of beliefs and limits. If I'm not good, does that mean I'm bad? If I don't do well in school, does that mean I've failed to live up to my potential? If I speak up or get angry for a good reason, does that still mean I'm misbehaving?

Labels create expectations.

Nicknames, and the feelings and expectations attached to them, are part of our identity. They define us—and quite possibly reflect behaviors or beliefs that confine us.

Think of the nicknames people use to highlight physical features. Labeling our size or body proportions may have a direct impact on body image. We can easily visualize what a person looks like based on these names:

Peanut, Pumpkin, Pipsqueak
Dumpling, Tubs, Chubs, Piglet
Beanstalk, Legs, Sticks
Runt, Shorty, Shrimp
Dumbo, Bigfoot, Four-eyes

These nicknames may seem cute, but when they're used to describe children still forming their self-image, they can lead to body image issues that might create mental and physical health concerns. Without meaning to, nicknames can create a sense of being *less than* acceptable.

We also label children with terms that personify behaviors. While those characteristics may reflect how children behave at specific times in their lives, these descriptive terms can become embedded in their language and minds. They could embrace behaviors associated with nicknames as truth and try to live up to them.

Think about how the following names create expectations of what someone is like:

    Crybaby, Clown, Chatterbox, Charmer
    Butterfingers, Bookworm, Dreamer
    Temperamental, Trouble, Tiger
    Goofy, Monkey, Mousy

Expectations shape identity.

Children are sponges. They absorb what they're told and behave the way they're expected to act. Those actions become habits and behaviors that persist into teen years and adulthood.

Limiting language often starts with good intention. We use seemingly innocent endearments to show affection. Yet because children instinctively seek parental approval, nicknames may suggest that they need to be sweet, kind, gentle, delicate, strong, athletic, or perfect:

    Sweetheart, Buttercup, Princess, Baby, Sugar
    Sunshine, Care Bear, Angel, Peach, Kitten
    Handsome, Champ, Prince, Ace, Slugger

The human brain acts as an observer. It classifies people as a shortcut to understanding who we are and where we fit into the world spinning around us. Our brains create boxes to classify us and then label those boxes for quick recall.

Nouns like mother, father, child, and parent are big boxes. Larger categories are subdivided by adjectives to refine the groups into manageable subsets. For example:

Strong boy	Silly girl
Slow student	Athletic child
Smart friend	Moody kid
Little guy	Mini me

Adjectives add another layer of labeling. Like nouns, when used consistently over time, adjectives define who we are . . . and quite possibly create expectations that could prevent us from seeing alternate possibilities for ourselves.

And it's not just names. Our lived experiences affect how we associate various words with our identity.

When my son was about six years old, we spotted a donkey at the farmers' market. Kyle had just learned that another name for donkey was *ass*, and he bounced with glee as he taught his mother this nugget of wisdom.

"I'm not swearing, Mom. That's really what a donkey is called."

My son was giddy with excitement—until we learned that the donkey's name was Buddy. Buddy was my son's nickname.

NICKNAMES CREATE ASS-UMPTIONS

"Buddy"   "Buddy"

You can imagine the shock and tears when my little boy thought his parents had been calling him an ass! Hearing the donkey's name changed how my son felt about himself in an instant. All because of a harmless nickname.

Limiting labels limit identity.

Nicknames may differentiate us from our formal identity or reinforce the images created by our names and our roles in family and community. They can have a powerful emotional influence on us, specifically because they are bestowed on us by the people closest to us. Nicknames become intimate identities that significantly impact our actions, behaviors, and choices—the ABCs of identity.

Growing out of nicknames is difficult, especially when we're mingling in the families or communities that bestowed them on us. We unconsciously resurrect the images associated with our nicknames when we are in these environments. They are, or were, our identity within the group.

A pause for thought before we leave this chapter:

> ### Recall how we live up to our labels and nicknames:
>
> Names are labels.
> Labels create expectations.
> Expectations shape identity.
> Limiting labels limit identity.

4. WE BECOME WHO WE EXPECT TO BE.

We weren't taught to show up.
We were taught to shut up. –Alicia Grayeb

Babies are born innocent.

Each breath we take brings new energy. Each movement we make is an experiment. Each sound we hear and each taste we experience engages our senses and provokes a reaction.

Each day is about exploring, learning, growing, and becoming. Our innate sense of curiosity introduces us to endless possibilities. Life is exciting, scary, surprising, and limitless.

How long we stay absorbed in curiosity, innocence, and exponential growth varies. What doesn't vary is that innocence doesn't last. As we grow and develop, we start to learn about cause and effect.

We learn crying gets attention and smiles make people coo at us. We learn hunger is physical and messing a diaper feels good—even though the person changing it may not have a happy face.

We start to associate actions with consequences:

Shampoo makes eyes water.

Running can lead to falling, and falling hurts.

Pulling the cat's tail makes the cat angry.

Writing on the wall with poo makes Mom angry.

Some of what we learn is necessary for our survival: clothing keeps us warm; food gives us energy; fire can burn. We learn what is acceptable and what is not, which means we learn about boundaries, expectations, and limits.

Worthiness is attached to words.

Words are powerful. They carry meaning and evoke emotional reactions. Take a few seconds to think about words that make you smile. And words that trigger doubt.

One of the earliest exposures we have to acceptable behavior comes in the form of language:

NO!
Stop!
Be quiet!
Bad!
Don't!

Language teaches and disciplines. It defines limits and boundaries that create expectations of what we can or can't, and should or shouldn't, do. Many admonitions are intended to protect and guide us, but body language, tone of voice, and impatience can lead us to associate our actions with unacceptable behavior.

Don't do that!
You're doing it wrong!
You can't do that!
Don't get too big for your britches!
WHO DO YOU THINK YOU ARE?

As young children, we can't separate our self-worth from our actions. We hear, see, and feel disapproval. We feel the shame of not being good enough.

Language itself isn't responsible for the confusion and chaos created by these warnings. Language was developed as a form of communication and connection. But limiting language is created by context. It's not just the words, it's the delivery and the body language. For example:

Are you SURE you can do this?

> Possible interpretation: *You don't think I can.*
> Possible reaction: *Maybe I can't.*

I wish you wouldn't . . .

> Possible interpretation: *I'm disappointing you.*
> Possible reaction: *I'm being bad/selfish.*

Why do you always . . .

>Possible interpretation: *I can't do anything right.*
>
>Possible reaction: *I'm a loser/incompetent idiot.*

Language can validate us or lead us to question our capabilities and choices. The impact of both limiting and empowering language depends on how close and intimate our relationships are with the people commenting on us and our actions.

Because human beings learn from repetition, the words we hear the most influence our early impressions about who we are. Words aren't merely a set of syllables, they create meaning.

Words become labels that create conscious or subconscious beliefs and biases. Those early impressions, whether positive or negative, shape us.

Labels identify us.

Many women have been taught to be quiet, to be good, and to be nice. When we step out of bounds and speak up, or when we defy cultural norms, we risk rejection. That fear can prevent us from making choices to fully express who we are. We let labels create our identity.

Labels may create a sense of individuality as well as a sense of belonging within our families, communities, and workplaces. But word labels also put us in boxes that make it easy for other people to establish our place within *their* world.

When word labels align with who we are and who we want to be, they give us permission to pursue and develop key aspects of who we are. However, if labels define us in a way that prevents us from growing, those labels can become cages that keep us from exploring possibilities.

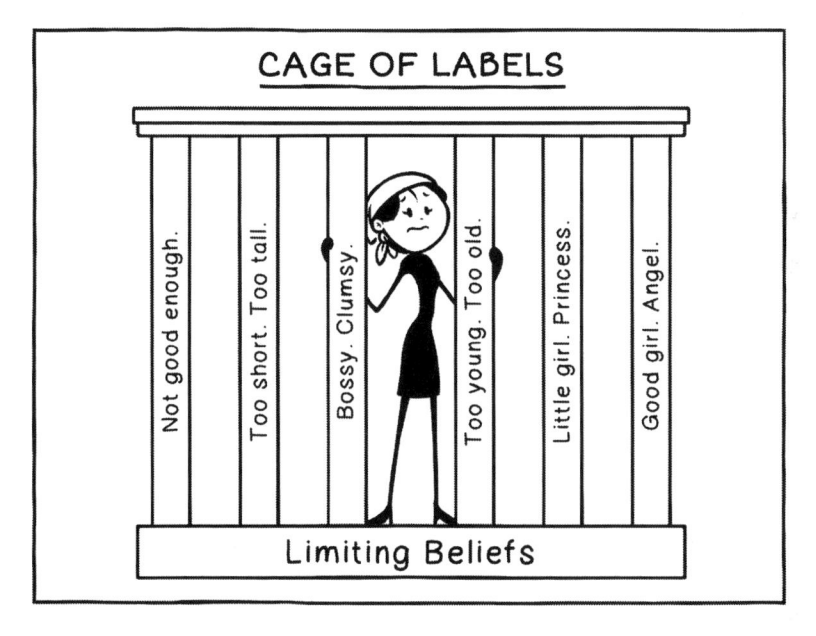

CAGE OF LABELS

Not good enough. Too short. Too tall. Bossy. Clumsy. Too young. Too old. Little girl. Princess. Good girl. Angel.

Limiting Beliefs

We live in a Cage of Labels.

The Cage of Labels consists of all the influences and expectations that hold us back. It typically develops over time, defining us and confining us to the personality and characteristics those labels represent. Those labels keep us trapped in the status quo and prevent us from becoming the best we can be.

The Cage of Labels reflects our public identity. So even when we look outside the cage, we see rules and boundaries that seem impossible to surmount—boundaries preventing us from trying to do anything more than meeting the expectations of what we *should* be doing.

We give in.

When we don't think we can do something, we don't try. When we don't believe we can live up to the expectations placed on us, we don't try.

When we don't believe we deserve more, or we don't believe we're worthy of more, we don't pursue more.

When we don't try, our growth stops. We reach the Expectations Ceiling.

A pause for thought before we leave this chapter:

> **Here's why we become who we expect to be:**
>
> ---
>
> Worthiness is attached to words.
> Labels identify us.
> We live in a Cage of Labels.
> We give in.

PART 2:

Why do we hold ourselves back?

> YOU ARE MORE POWERFUL THAN YOU THINK.
> DON'T DOUBT YOURSELF SO MUCH. —CATHY SWEET

The nightmare of rejection.

A picture triggered the shame of my nightmare.

I was in my early thirties and impulsively decided to fly to Calgary to surprise my parents for their anniversary. Mom and Dad were sorting old photographs on the dining room table when I arrived, and I wandered over to look. I picked up the picture of a woman in her wedding dress and, hands shaking, asked who she was.

"My mother," Dad said.

"I know her," I whispered.

"Impossible." Dad shook his head. "She died when I was four years old."

I collapsed on a chair. For decades I'd had a recurring dream. I was a child, running through a hayfield. Not a lovely meadow full of beautiful flowers, but a field of dry brown grass decaying in the wind. In my dream I was running toward a woman—the woman in the picture. The grandmother I'd never known.

Rather than a pristine wedding dress, in my dream my grandmother was wearing a plain dress with puffy sleeves, a soiled apron, and a frown. Her hands were locked on her hips, and I slowed as I approached her. She was obviously not happy to see me.

"What are you doing here?" she demanded.

I started to cry. I didn't know. I didn't even know where "here" was. All I knew was that I'd been lost in the tall grass, and she was the only person in sight. She sighed and bent over to pick me up, then gave me a quick hug.

"You don't belong here. Go back." Her voice was brittle. She set me down, turned me to face back the way I'd come, and pushed me away.

I'd had that dream—that nightmare of rejection—every night for as long as I could remember. It left me feeling unwanted. Like I wasn't worthy of attention. And now I was learning that I'd been rejected by my own grandmother!

I stared at the picture in my hands and, between sobs, explained the dream to my parents. Their reaction was unexpected. They looked at one another the way parents silently communicate with each other. Mom finally broke the silence.

"I guess the doctors were wrong. They said you wouldn't

remember anything."

They were referring to a surgery I'd had when I was eight years old... the first of four operations intended to correct my leg length difference. It was essentially a form of heart bypass surgery, even though my heart was okay. The doctors were experimenting, testing if extra blood flow would help my defective leg grow faster.

I have been told I was the youngest person in North America to have this type of surgery at the time. It was a complex procedure that involved rechanneling arteries and veins in my leg. Performed by a rotating team of surgeons, it took most of a day to complete.

And apparently, at some point a blood clot created a blockage and cut off oxygen. Nothing serious, the doctors had said. Nothing I would remember. They'd reassured my parents there would be no aftereffects.

Except the recurring dream I'd never understood.

My parents' revelation explained something else I'd never understood—why I have no memories of my early childhood. No hugs or laughter or parties or fun. My earliest memory is waking up in a pool of blood in the hospital after surgery. I'd never talked about that traumatic time because it was a terrifying memory. It wasn't something I wanted to dwell on. After all, who wants to say she remembers her childhood as a bloody mess?

But there I was, an adult, finding out I'd died more than twenty years earlier. The two strongest memories I had—being rejected *by this strange woman in a soiled apron and waking up to a bed full of blood—suddenly made sense.*

I had died. I had been reborn.

I started to wonder about the dream's meaning. I'd always interpreted being sent back as rejection, but maybe my grandmother had sent me back to live! Why did she want me to live? Was there a purpose to my life that I'd never embraced? Is that why the Universe kept sending me signals, like car crashes and illnesses, that reset my path from self-destruction to self-discovery?

I began questioning the sense of unworthiness that kept creeping into my choices. Perhaps it was time to appreciate all I had achieved and how much more I was capable of.

I stared at the picture of my grandmother and re-imagined the dream. She hadn't been rejecting me; she had sent me back to fulfill my life goals. My grandmother wanted me to know that I had a purpose. I had a reason to live.

Once I embraced the belief that my grandmother had sent me back to make a difference in the world, I never had the nightmare of rejection again.

5. BEING GOOD PREVENTS US FROM BEING GREAT.

The golden handcuffs of apparent success hold us back from pursuing real success. –Anne-Marie Warburton

My friend Kerry is an amazing project manager. She's so proficient that project leads constantly ask for her on their teams. They know she will make them look good.

And she will. She loves delivering excellent results. She loves the praise and appreciation . . . and as long as she calls herself a project manager, she will always be one. Which would be okay if that's what she wants. But it's not.

Kerry knows several project leads have gotten promotions, raises, and bonuses because of her work. She also knows they became leads partially because they stepped forward and asked for the opportunity.

What do you think would happen if next time a project came up,

Kerry presented herself as a candidate for project lead? Yes, the qualifications and skill sets differ from her current role. At the same time, if Kerry never sees herself as a project lead, she won't become one. She will limit herself by accepting the project manager label as her identity. She will wear the title and stay in the role until she no longer loves it.

Like Kerry, most of us need to give ourselves permission to grow. Perhaps we also need to give ourselves permission to reject the way other people limit us.

The need for acceptance shapes our choices.

There's a well-known theory called Maslow's Hierarchy of Needs[2] that outlines the importance of belonging on our sense of Self.

Abraham Maslow, an American psychologist, defined this hierarchy as five categories of needs: physiological, safety/security, love/belonging, esteem, and self-actualization. His treatise *Hierarchy of Needs: A Theory of Human Motivation*, first published in 1943, illustrates these needs, including how they motivate us, as a pyramid.

The most basic *physiological* needs are the first level. They provide the foundation for all our other needs. They are the primary needs required for survival: food, water, clothing, and shelter.

Once our primary needs are met, we begin to look for *safety and security*. Having a home and an income source provides us with stability and a way to maintain a continuous source of food, water, clothing, and shelter. Meeting this second layer of needs creates a safety net, supporting our health and wellness as well as our financial security.

Our basic needs must be satisfied before we can move up the pyramid to higher emotional needs. There may be some overlap, but we generally can't focus on intangible desires like love and belonging until we feel safe and secure in the knowledge our physical needs are met.

Love and belonging needs are the middle tier, the point where social needs become the focus of our attention. We want relationships. We want to be part of groups, to be intimate, and to have a sense of connection to our communities.

Why? Because the love and affection we receive from family and friends gives us a sense of acceptance and connection. Maslow believed we need love and belonging before we can feel good about who we are. It's the core from which confidence is built.

The next level on the pyramid is *esteem*, which Maslow called the emotional need for acceptance. As the word suggests, esteem is about feeling appreciated and respected. To achieve this state, we need both internal validation (self-esteem) and external recognition (acceptance).

When we have a strong sense of our abilities, we have more self-confidence and self-respect. Feeling good about our strengths, behaviors, and capabilities increases our pride in who we are and our sense of worthiness.

Recognition makes us feel valued.

We feel appreciated when others show us respect and acceptance. Recognition may be reflected in the status we have in society or by the attention we get in groups, communities, or relationships. It may be an award, a raise, a promotion, or an expression of gratitude.

The first levels of Maslow's Hierarchy are often referred to as *deficiency* needs. The concept of deficiency needs underlies what psychologists, coaches, and therapists often refer to as a *scarcity mindset*—the uneasy belief there isn't enough for everyone. Our underlying fear is that we may lose what we have achieved, and we may never have what we want.

We build our sense of self by using our skills and talents to accomplish goals, which helps create self-confidence. Gaining recognition for those achievements and contributions reinforces our self-esteem because it highlights how valuable and important we are to others.

This combination of internal and external worthiness nurtures positive emotions, which helps us continue to embrace challenges and grow. It's a path toward self-assurance and self-fulfillment.

Confidence comes with practice.

Building confidence takes effort. As Mayor Dawn Arnold says, confidence is a work in progress. It comes with practice and putting ourselves out there—seeing we can do hard things and acknowledging and remembering those achievements in the tough times. And it's vital for Dawn's role. She says, "Confidence is critical because if you're not confident, you can't do this job."

At the same time, Dawn knows that being mayor is not all that she is. "It's that whole thing around esteem," she explained. "I know the second I no longer have the title *mayor*, no one is going to take my call, so it is important to ensure that I remember who I am, what my values are, what I am really trying to accomplish, and why."

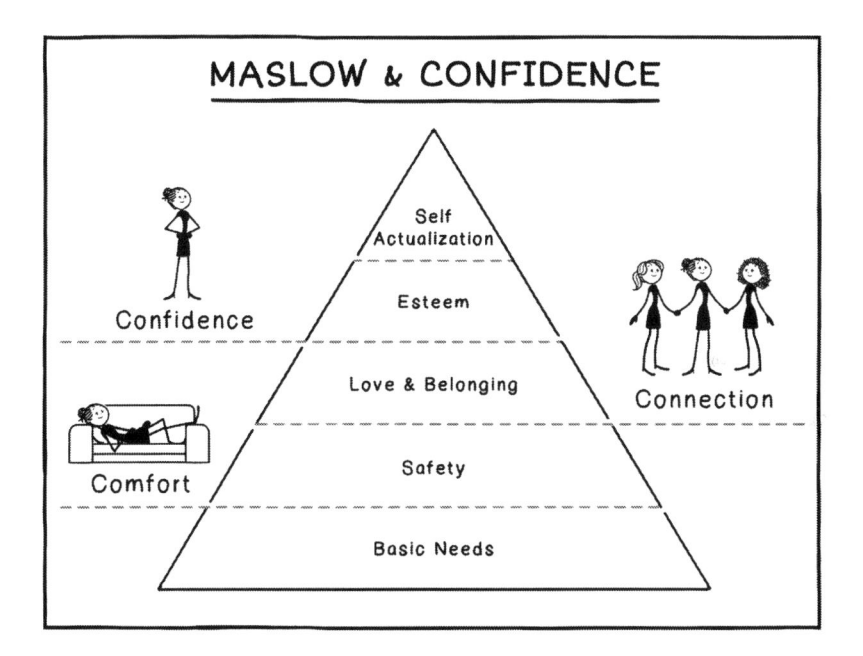

MASLOW & CONFIDENCE

- Confidence
- Comfort
- Self Actualization
- Esteem
- Love & Belonging
- Safety
- Basic Needs
- Connection

Dawn's comments reflect the balance most of us seek between self-esteem and external recognition. According to Maslow's philosophy, finding this balance is important because we can only explore the top need in the pyramid, *self-actualization,* once we have both self-esteem and recognition.

Self-actualization is a *being* need. Being needs reflect the personal and creative pursuits required to reach our full potential. We attain the *self-fulfillment* aspect of self-actualization once our other needs are met. Self-actualization is the point where we can do what we want to do—what we believe we are meant to do.

Self-fulfillment needs self-expression.

Self-fulfillment occurs when we are free to express our individuality and embrace our potential. The form this expression takes differs for each person: it may be through creativity, artistic endeavors, or optimizing talents and capabilities. Whatever form our expression takes, it is the culmination of our identity.

How do we reach the stage where we consciously and consistently choose to do what fulfills us? Belonging is such a strong need that we tend to minimize the potential for rejection. We hesitate to experiment and take risks. We fall back on our need for safety.

Fear, guilt, and doubt are humankind's safety anchors . . . they prevent us from setting out on what could be dangerous adventures. These voices urge us to sail quietly along, not rocking the boat. They encourage us to find comfort anchored in the safety of love and belonging.

But what if we do want more? How do we find the balance? How do we navigate the seas of unease and set off on journeys to become who we want to be . . . and still have welcoming homes to come back to?

Is it possible to balance belonging with being all we can be?

A pause for thought before we leave this chapter:

> **Recall how being good prevents us from being great:**
>
> ---
>
> The need for acceptance shapes our choices.
> Recognition makes us feel valued.
> Confidence comes with practice.
> Self-fulfillment needs self-expression.

6. FITTING IN PREVENTS US FROM BEING OURSELVES.

One of the biggest surprises in this research was learning that fitting in and belonging are not the same thing. In fact, fitting in is one of the greatest barriers to belonging. –Brené Brown

---

What's one of the first questions we ask when we are invited to an event? "What's the dress code?" We want to ensure we balance fitting in with showing up as individuals because our confidence and identity are emotionally connected to feelings of belonging. We care about what we wear because we want to be accepted.

We care about being accepted.

In many ways, men have it easy when it comes to clothes. They often show up in jeans and a Tee. Maybe a jacket. Women don't usually have such flexibility. We face internal and external expectations on how we should show up. As a result, we have more options. More choices and decisions. More angst.

Some women have core outfits or uniforms they wear but many of us stand in front of our closets and debate:

Do I want to wear this or that?
What color? What shoes? How much jewelry?
I don't know . . . how do I want to feel today?

The last question is the most important one. Clothing affects the way we feel about ourselves and how we think others will judge us. Which means clothing affects how we show up. Should we choose an outfit for fashion or fit? Do we pick a color because it flatters us or because it's in style?

We take time to be intentional about the clothes we wear, yet the most important thing we wear is something we often don't think about—our words. The words we wear when we talk about our personality, passions, dreams, and ambitions.

Word labels, like clothing labels, affect the way we feel, how we show up, and, consequently, how we connect with others. Connection helps channel acceptance, and acceptance by family, friends, and communities forms the backbone of our identity. Acceptance creates a safe space to express ourselves . . . within limits.

The desire to belong exerts an element of resistance to standing out as an individual, and the resulting tension can create emotional conflict. Imagine (or recall) being in a room where people stare at you. Where no one invites you to sit down or stay. You stand out. You are different.

You're dressed wrong. Whatever the reason, you feel like an outcast.

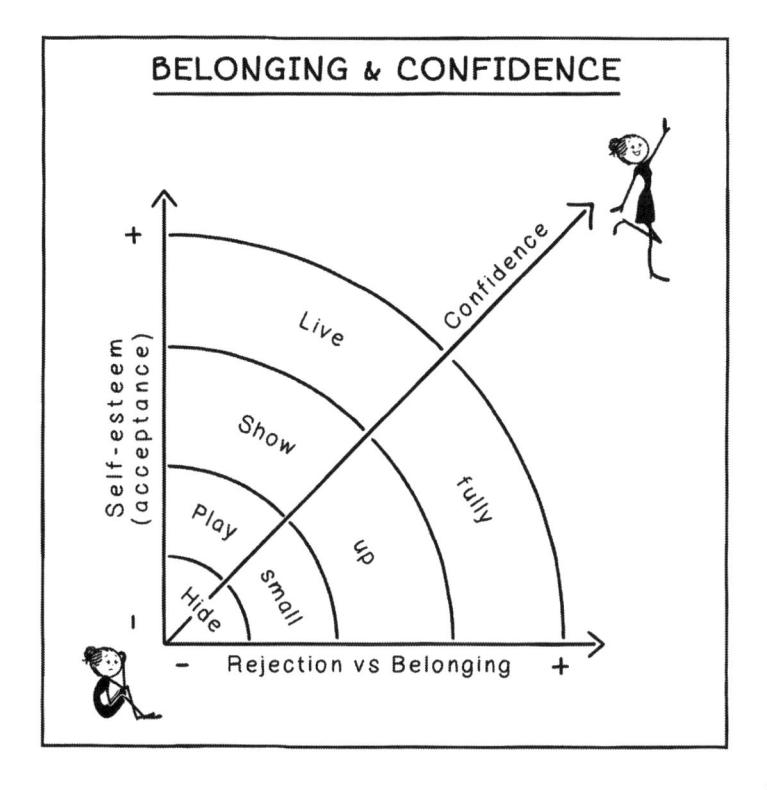

BELONGING & CONFIDENCE

Self-esteem (acceptance) vs *Rejection vs Belonging*

Zones from inner to outer: Hide, Play small, Show up, Live fully. Diagonal arrow: Confidence.

Now imagine walking into a room and being greeted by friends. The inviting energy inspires you to share, experiment, and be free to learn and grow. The sense of security attached to acceptance may encourage you to pursue your ambitions. Yet that same sense of security subtly encourages you to stay safely nestled in your home and community.

We question ourselves when we don't fit in.

We start to look for our defects, for the reasons why we aren't acceptable. We decide we have to change to belong. That desire to belong can threaten our sense of safety and comfort and cause us to hide our skills and talents. We might underperform at school so we don't stand out as *too smart*, as *brainiacs*, or as *teachers' pets*.

Having friends is a signal we are acceptable.

Finding friends and fitting in can mean accepting the limits—the rules—that a family, group, or community sets. In a community, those standards are typically based on similarities and an alignment of values. A book club assumes participants are readers interested in sharing their insights and opinions. Members who don't read the books or insist on talking about movies they saw may not be welcomed by more serious club members.

Even a place as welcoming as a retirement community has real or perceived limits, usually centered around people who no longer work full time. The community may not have rules about who can live there, but simple things like designing activities around residents who are available during the day limits participation opportunities for working residents.

These standards set the boundaries of expectations—the rules and guidelines regarding what we are supposed to do and to be. When we choose a community, we choose to adopt or accept these guidelines. However, when we are born into certain cultures, sent to particular schools, or raised in restrictive settings, we may be constrained by boundaries we don't want or didn't agree with. How much are we willing to give up to step into worlds where we feel we belong? How much do we unconsciously give up when we don't?

The nuances of language helped Alicia Grayeb choose self-expression. Her first language is Spanish, a musical love language steeped in culture. Her second language, English, exposed her to a different, bolder type of expression. She was only ten years old when she first experienced the cultural variances of these languages while attending a summer camp in Ireland. She recalls how happy she was speaking English because she could express herself more freely. Her dreams and ambitions found their voice.

Moving to the United Kingdom for her post-secondary education freed Alicia from conservative norms. While she still appreciates the beauty of her first language, it also triggers the cultural biases and limits she grew up with in Mexico. Speaking Spanish reminds Alicia of traditions and beliefs that silently undermine her sense of self. Using a bolder language gives voice to her aspirations, enabling her to pursue her passion for the environment and sustainability.

Belonging has a price.

Belonging is an innate yearning. We instinctively protect ourselves by seeking the balance between being who we are at the moment, becoming who we want to be in the future, and bridging belonging in the present. When the gap is too wide to straddle, one way forward is to find our own communities rather than being chameleons lost in the woods.

Alex Cattoni is a strong and independent woman, but she still experienced challenges with how to show up as herself. When she started her first consultancy business in 2012, she found herself in a male-dominated industry where traditional male standards set the tone. Like most people, she wanted to be liked, not judged, and she started second-guessing how she was showing up. She felt self-conscious about being her fierce, loud, feminine self.

At some point, Alex noticed there were two versions of herself: Business Alex and Real Alex. Business Alex was living up to other people's standards and making decisions based on what she thought she should do rather than assessing what felt right. When she realized those decisions often came back to bite her, Real Alex decided to *get over the BS* and fully own who she is. That's when she started the Copy Posse, which grew into a boutique agency, online academy, and global crew of copywriters.

She shared how she reached this awareness. "No matter what you do or don't do, there are going to be people who don't agree with you. Why would we let that hold us back? The clearer we are about who we are, the more we attract people who are like us, and then the more we feel like we belong."

By showing up true to who she is, Alex attracts people who understand and relate to her. Her biggest supporters, friends, and cheerleaders connect with Real Alex.

If we circle back to the need for belonging, we start to understand why our innate response to any situation is to find a way to fit in. Human beings need to belong. We need to feel loved. When we love ourselves and we feel loved by others, we have the confidence to grow and become the best we can be. We own our identity.

At the same time, the desire to belong—to be part of a family or group or relationship—can lead us to lose our identity. When we feel warm and comfortable, we might not want to rock the boat. We're not sure we want to lose what we've achieved, so we may compromise and conform. We give up little pieces of ourselves to fit in. To be accepted.

We compromise to fit in.

We start to listen to the inner voices that claw away at our self-esteem. The voices that ask us what we think we're doing, why we want more, why we can't be happy with what we have. We question why we're impatient or what makes us so self-assured and greedy. We hold back on expressing ourselves honestly in order to fit in, keep the peace, and make other people happy. We may even withdraw emotionally or compromise our values and principles.

Some of us recognize this tendency when we visit our parents or show up for high school reunions. We get greeted by nicknames that trigger old patterns. When we don those worn-out labels, our self-image is muddied by past experiences. Feelings we thought we'd outgrown emerge and trigger doubt, or even impostor syndrome. Our identity gets mired in stagnant thoughts and beliefs as we question whether we changed for the better or whether we're just kidding ourselves.

Other places where we hit ceilings of confidence are at points of success. When we are told, "You're really good at this, this is your future," we may resist anything that risks losing stature. We accept what we are good at as an upper limit and don't pursue ways to be great. We don't go for more; we go for safety.

The desire for belonging is a strong motivator. It leads to compromise. When we compromise, we shrink. We hide our accomplishments. We downplay our successes. We play small. We mute our voices and subdue our dreams and desires.

Does that matter? Yes, because we own our identity only when we consciously choose how we show up.

A pause for thought before we leave this chapter:

Recall how fitting in prevents us from being ourselves:

We care about being accepted.
We question ourselves when we don't fit in.
Belonging has a price.
We compromise to fit in.

7. BEING GOOD IS NEVER GOOD ENOUGH, AND PERFECTION IS IMPOSSIBLE.

Our expectation of perfection sets us up to fear failure. Yet there's acceptance in imperfection, where we can relax and start stepping into the self. –Jo Gillibrand

Life isn't a bowl of cherries. Where did that expression come from anyway? Cherries have pits. Life is full of uncertainties. There is no template for a perfect life. In fact, striving for perfection can ruin our lives.

Uncertainty brings new experiences, and we grow through those experiences. We learn about acceptance and rejection, which helps us develop capabilities and confidence. Yet many of us grow up with the belief that we have to be perfect the first time, every time. We accept standards—or even set ourselves standards—that are impossible to achieve.

Then we beat ourselves up with guilt and shame for not doing the impossible.

Renée Warren is a successful entrepreneur, running We Wild Women, a business that helps women entrepreneurs, and hosting *Into the Wild*, a top business podcast. She exudes confidence and capability, yet one of her biggest challenges has been managing guilt around parenting. Like many of the women she coaches, Renée juggles balancing her own needs and desires with the external expectations of women still evident today. Renée knows her husband doesn't feel guilty about his choices and actions, and she'd love to experience that kind of freedom from pressure.

"Women are supposed to work like they don't have children and mother like they don't work outside the home," she says. "Fathers don't face that expectation, so they have it easy, comparably."

Those external expectations feed our inner doubts, and at times our inner voices can be incessant. When Dawn Arnold won the race for mayor, her father told her, "That's really great. Now don't screw up." It wasn't the most celebratory response, yet it wasn't surprising. While Dawn's parents had supported her ideas and ambitions—partly because they couldn't stop her—they had always cautioned her not to screw up.

This perfection script still loops on repeat in Dawn's head, yet in many ways it has helped her. She consciously set perfection as a goal rather than a limit, which prepared her for her role and for being scrutinized as a woman in the mayor's role.

We can't win.

Despite all our worry and efforts, it seems nothing we do is good enough. We're trying to behave how we were taught to. We're trying to do what we're told we should do. Yet we still feel we're not good enough.

How can we be? We can never be enough if we're stretching ourselves to the limits of possibility by trying to live up to other people's expectations instead of creating our own lives and visions.

How many of us grew up believing we could never meet our parents' standards?

I was taught to be good . . . so I couldn't talk back even if the adult was saying something wrong.

I was supposed to be quiet and not have an opinion . . . but then I'd be told to think for myself.

I wasn't supposed to think I was better than others . . . yet I was supposed to get better marks because I was smarter than they were.

I had to be an A+ student. An A wasn't good enough.

I was expected to be at the top of my class . . . but I wasn't supposed to brag about it.

I was taught to follow the rules of the church and be kind to everyone . . . but not forget that my religion was better than other religions.

I was supposed to follow traditional career/life paths for a working man's daughter (finish school, get married, have children) . . . and yet make the most of my talents.

> **THE BURDEN OF PERFECTION**
>
> You should...
> Behave   Be good
> Respect others
> Do more
> Do better
> You can't
> Why risk?
> Don't be selfish
>
> Dreams

We are supposed to do what we're told, make others proud, and not create waves. We are never enough because we're trying to do the impossible. We're trying to be who other people tell us we should be.

We are supposed to succeed . . . but only in the shadows.

Comparison is a confidence killer. Many of the women I talked to detailed how they were compared to siblings, cousins, neighbors, and friends. Compared and found lacking on some dimension. Despite any achievements they may have had in academics or sports or community involvement, their efforts weren't considered up to par in at least one area. The bottom line was that nothing they did was good enough because they couldn't be perfect at everything.

Anne-Marie Warburton grew up with four sisters and a brother. On the surface, her parents were supportive. They wanted their children to go to university and have more than what they had. Yet, like many parents, they never told Anne-Marie they were proud of her. In fact, they did the opposite. Anne-Marie's parents compared her to her sister, who was strong in the arts. Those comparisons minimized Anne-Marie, making her feel inadequate. Ironically, Anne-Marie's success as a custom jewelry designer and business owner draws on her strong artistic and creative talents.

Like many of her generation, Anne-Marie was taught that the women's lane was clearly marked. She could be a nurse, teacher, flight attendant, or mother. The fact that she was intelligent and ambitious didn't matter; her choices were dictated to her. As a result, Anne-Marie believed what she wanted didn't matter—and, therefore, neither did she. "I felt it didn't matter whether I was happy. My role was to make other people happy, but no matter how hard I tried, it was something I could never achieve."

My sister, Gail Blashyn, and I reflected on this one night over a glass of wine. She explained, "I wanted to make our parents happy, and I tried. I loved Mom and Dad, and I knew they loved me. I didn't want to risk that love, so I kept trying to find the 'mystical me' that would make them happy."

That mystical girl masked the outgoing adventurer who loved to dance and wanted to explore the world. Adventurous Gail wilted as Good Daughter Gail tried to behave in ways she hoped would make her parents tell her they were proud of her—tell *her*, not others.

Estelle Doiron, founder and CEO of Koffee Beauty, was a straight-A student who fell in love with sales when she was still in high school. Growing up, she'd done endless rounds of fundraising to support her participation in sports and activities, and the art of sales excited her. She knew she wanted to pursue it as a career. But her decision to enter community college to study sales confused her teachers and parents. People repeatedly questioned her decision. "Estelle, you're one of the smartest ones here. Why go to college when you should be in university?"

But Estelle didn't want a business degree, she wanted to focus on further developing her sales skills. She stood up for herself and pursued studies in sales. Today, she celebrates her choice. Launching a beauty product into a competitive space is a challenging venture, and Estelle's sales acumen is one of the biggest contributors to her success.

How often do our choices and actions reflect who we are or what we truly want?

The pressure for perfection destroys confidence.

Even when we know we're holding back or being held back, the pressure for perfection looms over us. The rules and restrictions that controlled us as children hover like thunderclouds, continuing to threaten us as adults.

Holding back is a learned response that undermines our confidence and how we feel about ourselves. We start to listen to comments about who we are, and we question what we should or shouldn't do. We may start to believe we're not enough, that we're nowhere near perfect, and we don't deserve more. This script of imperfection often leaves us subject to pressure from other people.

Tammy Price intuitively knew she was not in a good relationship, but when she finally found the courage to stand up for herself, she discovered her happiness didn't count. She recalls a particular evening when her fiancé was irritated because she was unavoidably late getting home, which meant they would be late for an event. Even though the delay wasn't her fault, he got physical with her when they were in the car.

It wasn't the first time he'd done it. Tammy had justified his actions before, taking on the blame and trying to do better. But being blamed for something out of her control was the last straw. She'd had enough. When her fiancé pulled up to a stop sign, she took off her engagement ring, threw it on the dashboard, and jumped out of the car. Then she ran for the safety of home.

Except she didn't find the refuge she was looking for. She was crying in her room when her father knocked on the door and told her to go downstairs and talk to her fiancé.

"I told Dad I was done. I'd had enough. My father's response: 'Well, do you want to be a spinster for the rest of your life?'"

Tammy suspected her dad knew this man was being abusive, so what he was saying was, "You're never going to get anyone any better than that. You don't deserve anything more."

That interaction crushed Tammy's spirit. She relented, and less than a year later she was walking down the aisle to marry a man who didn't value her as a person. It would take time before Tammy finally reached a place where she believed she deserved more and found the courage and strength to leave the marriage.

We need permission to believe we are enough.

Too many women abandon their dreams and their sense of self under the pressure of parental influence. It's hard to value yourself when the person you look to for support crushes your sense of worthiness and scoffs at your ambitions.

Edye Hoffmann is a compassionate and intelligent woman who is changing the world of dementia and dementia care. Yet she too had a rocky road to her destiny. A high school dropout, she left home and started working at seventeen. Smart and determined, she soon recognized the value of a higher education. However, she needed financial support to go to university, and her father sabotaged her education plans by refusing to sign the loan papers. "He asked me why I would want more than he had."

Edye's father tried to quell her ambitions, but he didn't succeed. Ultimately, her skills and capabilities caught the attention of a guidance counselor and a stranger, both of whom saw her potential. Having people believe in her gave Edye the impetus to follow her dreams. With their support and guidance, she eventually got her degree and now drives innovation in supporting families affected by dementia.

Edye had to find alternate sources of inspiration and support to enable her to reach beyond the limits established by her parents. More importantly, she had to find the courage to believe in herself and give herself permission to move beyond her parents' expectations.

A pause for thought before we leave this chapter:

Here's why being good is never good enough, and perfection is impossible:

We can't win.
We are supposed to succeed . . . but only in the shadows.
The pressure for perfection destroys confidence.
We need permission to believe we are enough.

8. WANTING MORE IS SEEN AS SELFISH.

*Don't wish for something—want it.
Wanting is asking for what you deserve;
wishing is merely suggesting it would be nice.* –Dr. Julia Sen

---

You're frustrated, restless, stressed, lost, overwhelmed, fed up—or maybe bored out of your mind. Maybe you've had a taste of adventure and achievement and now you can't be satisfied with anything less.

You know you want more than what you have—more time, more freedom, more money, more challenge, more adventure, more love, more fulfillment, more space to think and dream, more of more. BUT . . .

Responsibilities control your life. You have so many commitments. You're good at what you currently do. People rely on you. You have family, friends, and your future to think about. You don't have the time or money to chase an adventure, a long shot, or a silly dream.

Wanting more is a risk.

How could you possibly leave what's working well? What if you are wrong? What would everyone think? Maybe you should just be content. Play it safe. EXCEPT . . .

There's something calling you. There's a restlessness that won't settle. There's an injustice you can't tolerate. There's a legacy you want to leave. A vision you want to ignite.

You know you can *do* more. You know you can *be* more. You just have to figure out *how*. What do you need to do to step into *more*? Who do you have to *be*? How do you *find* yourself?

Pause on that thought. Why do you have to *find* yourself? Touch your face with your hand—you're right there. You don't need to be found. You need to be *released*.

What would happen if you let go of the *shoulds* that create huge shadows where your heart and soul live? What if you only need to become more of who you are at your core, rather than force-fitting yourself into the persona others have designed for you?

By definition, desire means we want more. We long for more. Growth starts when we challenge the mindsets holding us back. What would your world look like if you expected you could achieve your dreams?

What if you said, "I can do this"?

Growing up, psychologist Julia Sen didn't dream of being a ballerina or a princess. Just the opposite—she was a high-energy tomboy who didn't like dresses. But she did dream of baseball. She *loved* baseball, even though it was a passion that didn't align with her cultural norms. But she found a way around those expectations.

Julia had a gift that enabled her to circumvent tradition. She was an innate problem-solver. Whether it was helping friends or fiddling with machines, fixing things came naturally to Julia. Not only did she enjoy problem-solving, but her family also rewarded her for it. The more she was praised for solving problems and resolving issues, the more she embraced her gift.

Without realizing it, Julia developed skills and attitudes that created a unique advantage for her. As her family looked more and more to her for answers, her expectations of what she could do expanded. She was empowered to make choices, and she embraced the opportunities this created. Problem-solving gave Julia confidence in her ability to make her own decisions, without being constrained by the traditional limits of a South Asian female.

Sharon Preszler also had a passion for baseball. She was lean and athletic, with a strong, competitive spirit and a good arm. But those qualities didn't mean she was welcomed to the sport. People repeatedly told her she didn't belong on the ball field. Not because she wasn't good—but because she was a girl. Sharon was only ten when she first experienced this bias.

Some girls would have been discouraged, especially at this young age, but Sharon's mother went to bat for her. She told Sharon she could do anything a boy could do, and she demonstrated her beliefs by helping Sharon get on the Little League baseball team. With her mother's support, Sharon learned to challenge perceived limits and pursue her dreams. The belief that she could soar if she wanted to no doubt helped Sharon become the first female F-16 fighter pilot in the USA.

Our worthiness is challenged.

Sadly, many of us are brought up believing that wanting more is selfish.

As a child, Stephanie Major believed she was special. She thought she was a magical person meant to do great things. But the world she grew up in didn't support that image of Stephanie. Instead, she experienced criticism and neglect. Reality conflicted with Stephanie's sense of who she was. She believed she was a good person. She sensed magic at her core, but that precious part of her was slowly being eroded by the people she trusted to love her and look after her.

She remembers her confusion. "I actually started to hate the part of me that thought I was meant for more. I remember being a kid and I would do this thing—I'd crawl up to the sink and stare into the mirror, looking for that light, that magic in my eyes. I needed the magic to pull me forward and keep me going."

Stephanie admits there were times she snubbed the sparkle. "I cursed the thing that was telling me I was more, because I knew believing in it would end up hurting me. I'd get filled up with hope or I'd see a sparkle, and then I'd go back into my real world and it didn't make sense. I was mad at myself for wanting to believe. I hated myself for wanting to be more."

If you met Stephanie Major today, you'd know she's embraced her magic. She is living intentionally, designing a life that brings joy and play to each part of her: the inner child, the present woman, and the future self. But it was a struggle, with years spent in hiding. Since young Stephanie couldn't make sense of her real world, she escaped into her imagination. She instinctively protected herself by getting lost in books and art where the real world didn't exist.

Now Stephanie sees those years as gifts that helped her explore her artistic and intuitive strengths. She's doing things she always wanted to do and things she never thought possible. "I'm being in my body, feeling my emotions, loving myself unconditionally, expressing my thoughts and ideas."

Leaning into her creative source led Stephanie to greater confidence and opened the door to finding the magic she believed in—being electrically alive. Creating art or, as she says, "Living as if I am art."

The truth is, we're conditioned to show up in ways that make us acceptable. We compromise to meet other people's expectations of what's appropriate. On the flip side, when we believe in our own worthiness, we show up with confidence.

A sense of self-worth is one of the key characteristics among women who intentionally step into their identity. So how did they develop that sense of self-worth? What were the roles of their parents, teachers, family, community? Were these women born with a strong sense of self, or did the encouragement they received growing up create a sense of worthiness?

Many of the women I spoke with credited their mothers with giving them encouragement to pursue their dreams. Some benefited from father figures who didn't judge them as *less than* because they were female. Others had teachers who reinforced their love for learning and helped them embrace their desires and passions.

These women felt empowered because people close to them supported their dreams and ambitions. Women who believed they could achieve what they wanted were willing to pursue their goals. They accepted the challenge and the work. They also gave themselves permission to let go of relationships with people who were not aligned with their goals.

Many of them admitted they sometimes struggled with doubt and loneliness, but they continued to fight for what they wanted. They sought colleagues, mentors, and people with similar dreams and ambitions to guide them and help them navigate the rough waters. Their confidence and presence came from making choices that honored their gifts and their dreams.

Were they lucky? If you define luck as an inner drive that fires choices and actions, then yes, they had luck on their side. A spirit of creating possibilities kept them going even when they had challenging childhood experiences or relationships with people who tried to mold them into *acceptable* personas. In many cases, their biggest hurdles were resisting the internal and external voices that said they couldn't do something.

Veronica Piacek had great role models in her immigrant parents. She watched them learn a new language, start a business, and adapt to a new homeland. They didn't say they couldn't do something—they said they had to *learn how to* do it. By showing their children how to stand up for themselves and pursue their goals, Veronica's parents set a powerful example of taking responsibility.

Those early lessons encouraged Veronica to take responsibility for her future. She'd started to study health sciences because she knew it would please her mother to see one of her children with a profession in health care. She soon realized health sciences didn't interest her; she didn't want a career in that field. She started working for her father while she was studying and discovered how much she enjoyed the complexity and opportunity of the business world.

Pivoting to business school, Veronica found her passion: she fell in love with marketing. It exposed her to a range of ideas and allowed her to tap into the creative side she had put on hold when she was pursuing health sciences.

Marketing was an exciting, highly competitive career path with endless opportunities. Rather than letting the competitive aspect dissuade her, Veronica decided to intentionally design her career. She embraced responsibility for her choices and sought out opportunities that allowed her to grow. Her focus on growth taps into one of Veronica's key philosophies: she never underestimates her ability to learn things she's not good at. Fittingly, one of her favorite lines is "I can learn that."

Our voices control our choices.

According to baseball-loving Sharon Preszler, our choices are the most powerful indicators of our commitment to our dreams. In her keynote speeches, Sharon notes our choices are influenced by the voices we listen to, and we can consciously choose which ones we hear. "We get to decide who's inside our heads."

VOICES & CHOICES

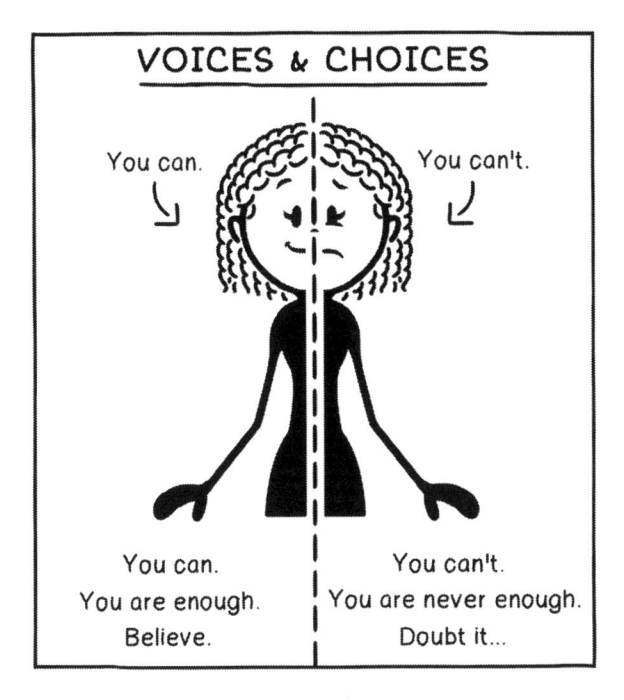

You can. ↙   You can't. ↙

You can.
You are enough.
Believe.

You can't.
You are never enough.
Doubt it...

Sharon's career was defined by her choices. She knew she wanted to be a pilot, but she couldn't afford training. Instead of being deterred, she enrolled in the military, prepared to embrace military discipline in exchange for training. The catch was, very few pilot training spots were available to women because of regulations restricting women from fighting on the frontline. As a result, Sharon was consigned to being a navigator.

Impatient to move ahead, Sharon decided to invest her savings in private pilot lessons. Having pilot training under her wings created a forward momentum path. By being proactive and resourceful, Sharon had demonstrated she was a solid candidate for fighter pilot training, and she achieved her dream.

At twenty-seven, Sharon became the first female F-16 fighter pilot in the USA. She was also the first woman to fly combat missions and instruct on the F-16. She could have stayed in the armed forces longer and risen higher in the ranks but being a Colonel wasn't important to Sharon. She retired from the Air Force at forty-one. By that time she had a child, and quality of life mattered more to her than stature.

By choosing to be a pilot and then a fighter pilot, Sharon hadn't followed a traditional career path for women, so it wasn't surprising that she decided she didn't have to follow the traditional military career path either.

In a similar manner, Lori Olson set her own bar for success. Lori is a respected trainer in software and app development and a legend in the Calgary developer community. She's built a successful career in computers, even though it wasn't her first choice. Her dream career was astrophysics, but according to the high school guidance counselor, there wouldn't be jobs available for Lori there. Nor, in his opinion, would her second career choice, geophysics, be an appropriate calling for a young woman. Why? Because geoscientists in the oil industry work in the field. He may have meant well, but he made assumptions about what Lori could or shouldn't do because she is female.

Since she loved logic, problem-solving, and exploring possibilities, computer science was the next best match to Lori's skills. Once she made this career choice, Lori committed to becoming the best programmer she could be.

Lori intentionally designed her career. She wanted to become a professional developer and trainer, so she consciously chose to raise her profile in the industry. She fixed projects that had tanked and chose challenges with high demands. She made sure she was noticed, not for being a woman, but for being a damn good developer.

It may appear that the Glass Ceiling didn't exist for these women, and in a sense, it didn't. They stepped through the looking glass, ignoring the limiting beliefs that hold others back. They set high expectations for themselves, and they gave themselves permission to go for what they wanted.

These examples make apparent that our career and life choices are affected by what options we believe are available to us. The voices in our heads tell us what we can expect, and those expectations affect what we accept and what we do.

How do we manage those voices? By changing the words, the stories, and the limits.

Our expectations about what we can and can't do—or do and don't deserve—affect our subconscious thoughts. And we know how powerful the subconscious is in forming our mindset around what's possible.

If we aim low and think small, we achieve small wins. If we aim high and think big, we make greater strides. We do bigger things. How do we learn to think bigger? How do we learn to increase our expectations of what's open to us?

We allow ourselves to dream. We give ourselves permission to believe in our dreams. We explore possibilities. We talk about, and ask about, possibilities. We believe in possibilities.

If we don't dream, we decay. We live in the status quo, confined to the limits other people put on us. If we want to grow, if we want to change the world, if we want to transform lives . . . then we need to believe we can.

Choice is the source of our power.

We must give ourselves permission to go for what we want. If we want to change the way other people see us, we must change the way we see ourselves. We must stop accepting limits other people place on us. It's our choice.

A pause for thought before we leave this chapter:

Here's why wanting more is seen as selfish:

Wanting more is a risk.
Our worthiness is challenged.
Our voices control our choices.
Choice is the source of our power.

PART 3:

How do we find ourselves?

> WE HAVE A LIMITED NUMBER OF MOMENTS IN LIFE.
> WE NEED TO RESPECT THOSE MOMENTS IF WE WANT TO ACHIEVE
> SOMETHING IN OUR LIFE. –PATRICIA GAGIC

I'll have a divorce with my hamburger.

The big Chevy was coming down the hill too fast for the icy road conditions. I prayed it wouldn't skid.

My prayers weren't answered. My baby blue Comet and my illusions of a quiet, predictable life were completely crushed—all because of a hamburger.

Ten minutes earlier my coworker and I had been sitting in the lunchroom. We looked at our boring sandwiches and impulsively decided to drive to Peter's Diner for "the best burgers" in Calgary. The most direct route took us up narrow Centre Street Bridge, so when the big gray car lost control and swerved toward us, there was no way to avoid it. We were trapped between the Chevy and the bridge railing.

The collision crushed the front of my car, demolishing the hood and pushing the driver's side fender into the engine. There were no airbags back then, so my friend flew into the dashboard and the window shattered on top of her. She was covered in broken glass and bruises. My face slammed against the steering wheel and the sound of my nose breaking popped in my ears.

Since I'd been braking when the car careened into us, my right leg was jammed between the steering column and the brake pedal. I couldn't move. I vaguely remember a paramedic holding my hand as firemen freed me.

My leg wasn't broken, although, in retrospect, a break might have healed faster. When the impact buckled the floor, it forced the foot on the brake into an unnatural angle, tearing a multitude of muscles in both my foot and the back of my leg. The pain screamed all the way up my spine.

I don't remember much from the first few days after the accident because I was high on pain relievers. But as the weeks dragged on, I found myself lying on the sofa at home, staring at the ceiling. My husband maintained his normal routine. He'd wake up, go to work, then play bridge or retire to his study in the evenings.

Before the accident, my own routine existed in parallel to his. I would come home from work, make supper, clean up, prepare lunches, then attend classes or study for the commerce degree I was completing at night school.

Hubby managed okay after the accident. He ate casseroles and sandwiches our families and friends dropped off. He set out trays for me before going to work, knowing one of our mothers would check in on me. Except for having to heat his own meals, he didn't really notice any changes. And he either didn't see or didn't acknowledge how much I was struggling.

I tried to be brave. I'd experienced a lot of physical pain from my childhood surgeries, so I could cope with the numbing headache and the searing pain in my leg. But the sharp stab of emotional agony debilitated me. I was a wreck.

I couldn't work. I couldn't go to classes. I couldn't study or watch TV because I couldn't wear glasses on my broken nose. I read a bit, but not enough to distract me from the empty echo in my home. The activities that had kept me from thinking about my life evaporated when I came home from the hospital. I was forced to face reality.

I had been married for three years. Against my father's wishes, I had walked down the aisle shortly after I turned nineteen—not because I was madly in love, but because I didn't know how to say no when my boyfriend proposed. Both loners, we'd met through a youth church group when I was fifteen. We'd been going steady for three years when he gave me a ring at Christmas. It wasn't the most romantic proposal; he simply handed me a present in front of his family on Christmas Day. When I opened it and saw the ring, I didn't want to destroy their excitement by admitting I wasn't ready to settle down. We had a small wedding the following summer, and it had been okay.

***Okay** being the operative word. There was nothing magical or romantic about our life together. I didn't have a marriage; I had a roommate.*

Not that I had expected a storybook romance. I'd grown up knowing I wasn't the most desirable woman. I am covered in scars from all my surgeries. My spine is crooked, and my feet are two different sizes. In one sense, I'd felt lucky that anyone wanted to marry me at all.

But as weeks and months dragged on after the accident, the sham of my marriage taunted me. No matter how hard I tried to rationalize being married was better than being single, I couldn't escape the loneliness that enveloped me when my husband walked out the door every morning and most evenings.

I couldn't blame him. About the only thing we'd ever done together was visit our families. I had tried to join him for bridge nights, but I hated how prescriptive and competitive the game was. He wasn't into yoga or hiking or anything related to the outdoors I loved. The truth was, we had nothing in common. In fact, when we took marriage counseling months later, the therapist said she didn't know how we ever got together in the first place. No matter what she suggested we try, we couldn't find a connection. Nothing was holding us together except our wedding certificate.

A piece of paper wasn't enough. At twenty-three, I finally decided I deserved more from life than pain and loneliness. I left my marriage.

That decision triggered a domino effect. While my devout Catholic father hadn't wanted me to get married, he was quick to point out getting a divorce wasn't an option for a good Catholic girl. He wouldn't accept being unhappy as a reason to commit a "sin." Not only did divorce violate his religious principles, but it also set a bad example for my seven sisters.

My father stood in his integrity. He disowned me. He forbade me to see my sisters. At a time in my life when I needed love and support, I was set adrift. Not because Dad didn't love me, but because at that point in time, he himself didn't realize happiness was something we all deserved.

Ironically, disowning me was the best thing my father could have done for me. It set me free.

Because I wasn't allowed to go home, I no longer had to live up to my parents' expectations of right and wrong. And when the Church excommunicated me, I was freed from the strict disciplines of a conservative religion. No one was telling me what to do anymore. No one was telling me how to behave.

I started to make choices for myself. I set my own goals and expectations of what I could and couldn't do. Yes, I messed up. A lot. I cried. A lot. And I laughed, played, and grew a lot.

I didn't know it at the time, but the day I decided to leave my marriage was the first time I made the choice to own my life and my identity.

9. TRAUMA AND TROUBLE FORCE US OUT OF OUR COMFORT ZONES.

Drama and trauma incite connection, and connection helps us understand and heal the past so we can move toward a better future. –Tammy Price

---

You've hit the ceiling.

The Glass Ceiling holding you back from where you want to go professionally.

The Education Ceiling stopping you from career opportunities.

The Health Ceiling curtailing your activities and adventures.

The Financial Ceiling preventing you from investing in your future.

The Expectations Ceiling keeping you from living fully expressed.

Maybe you've reached a plateau where you're secure, safe, and successful. Yes, there's a gnawing need in your belly, but you can't think about it right now. You carry a cloak of responsibility, and it's smothering the fires of passion in your soul. You no longer know who you are or what you want.

Getting caught up in the routines of life and the distraction of day-to-day living is easy. We absorb the *shoulds* and *musts* inherited from our upbringing and bury the thoughts and dreams of wanting more.

Until something challenges us.

Have you ever wondered why successful entrepreneurs, accountants, and doctors walk away from their careers and embark on entirely different journeys? Or why a personal crisis is often described as "life changing" and "the best thing that happened to me"?

Events like my car accident interrupt complacency. They break the routines that keep us stuck in a rut on a narrow track.

We expect life to have its ups and downs, but sudden changes or events interrupt the patterns that keep us tied to our day-by-day existence. We can't predict a crisis, so the lack of control it spawns plays havoc with our minds—especially when we experience sudden, emotionally significant changes. We're forced to think and make decisions we may not be prepared to make . . . and may not even want to think about.

Many of the women I talked to made significant life changes when something forced them out of their comfort zones. In my case, it was car accidents (yes, more than one) that stopped my headstrong rush and made me reassess what I was doing with my life.

We weren't always averse to those changes. Sometimes random dreams and thoughts had been nibbling at our consciousness for a while, but we couldn't justify action. It's amazing how well we rationalize that being unhappy is not enough of a reason to upset our patterns of life. But when something dramatic happens, easy excuses don't hold up.

What level of discontent or frustration is necessary before we deliberately take a step toward changing our lives? What makes us choose to stay on the hamster wheel going round and round and round, or grab onto something and pull ourselves out?

Disruption triggers transformation.

Drama, trauma, and turmoil are some of the most common triggers. They may happen quickly or slowly build to a crisis point.

Jo Gillibrand's journey into self-awareness took on momentum when her marriage unexpectedly ended. The end of any relationship is upsetting, but when it's a surprise, it can shatter a woman's sense of self-confidence. While the hurt was real, Jo's response to being suddenly single helped her realize what a strong and resilient woman she is.

As a mindfulness coach, Jo understands the way our thoughts and beliefs influence our actions, and she highlights the importance of the support and nourishment we receive from friends when major changes interrupt our lives. She says she didn't get through the changes alone.

She turned to friends.

"True friends take care of your confidence when it's so shattered you can't see it yourself, and they shine a light on a future where you not only recover, but also thrive."

Jo didn't intentionally choose to become single, but when it happened, she made deliberate choices to guide her as she adapted to her new life.

Sharon Preszler made a major life and career decision when her son was diagnosed with leukemia. Instead of taking a promotion to Colonel, the fighter pilot left the Air Force to become a commercial pilot and be closer to home.

Family was also a trigger for Edye Hoffmann. She always knew she would be involved in community work, but her focus unexpectedly narrowed when she became a caregiver to her mother-in-law. She spent years creating support mechanisms to help her mother-in-law continue to function and enjoy life despite encroaching dementia. Being able to help her was rewarding, but Edye grew frustrated after years of navigating through the progression of the condition and seeing the lack of community support for people with dementia and their caregivers. Clearly there was a massive need for support at the community level, but no one was providing it.

"I was sick and tired of being sick and tired of the fact there was no support, so I decided to do something about it," Edye said.

At times, our emotional or physical health is what sparks change. Medical intuitive Tammy Price, marketing coach Kelsey Reidl, community builder Sally Ng, and contemporary artist Patricia Gagic are just a few of the women who surprised people when they left financially secure, good-paying corporate positions. They were good at their work. They were appreciated by their clients and managers. But what may have been good jobs for other people were not aligned with the dreams and ambitions these women had. The misalignment manifested in stress, health issues, and a feeling they could be wasting their lives.

If our identity is associated with the roles we play and the work we do, what happens to us if we don't like those roles or our work?

IDENTITY CRISIS

What's my purpose?

Who am I?

What's wrong?

Who do I want to be?

Why can't I be happy?

Why am I here?

Uncertainty invites an identity crisis.

"Identity crisis" is another one of those phrases with multiple meanings. Does an identity crisis come from not knowing who you are, not liking who you are, or simply wanting to be more of who you are?

Any or all of the above.

Essentially, an identity crisis is the uncertainty and confusion arising when a person's sense of identity becomes clouded. While identity evolves as we change and grow, when significant or unexpected things disrupt our lives, we lose our groundedness. We may question our sense of self and our place in the world.

Anne-Marie Warburton recalls how she loved working as a merchandiser for an international retail store. Imagine her shock when she returned from a three-day work trip to New York City to discover the company she worked for had been acquired in a hostile takeover—and her job had been eliminated. Losing her job would have been traumatic enough, but the impact on her self-esteem was compounded by two other blows: her marriage was ending, and she'd received a recent diagnosis of a medical condition in her legs. Her marriage, her work, and her self-image were all disrupted at the same time.

"It ended up being the best thing that could have happened to me. I had terrible self-esteem up until that point. I had a very low opinion of myself, and I was also hiding out, not being myself. This series of events gave me the freedom to find myself and grow as a person. It was exciting and life changing."

Job loss and divorce are considered traumatic events. Some other situations that may contribute to us questioning our identity and future include:

- △ Moving, traveling, or leaving home
- △ Education, experiences, or exposure to something new
- △ Illness or injury
- △ Marriage or a change in the family unit or dynamic
- △ Having children, losing a loved one, or becoming an empty nester
- △ Frustration or disillusion with work or relationships
- △ A strong urge to take action to fix something

Not all these events are unplanned. Not all are crises. But they create disruption, which can consciously or unconsciously give us permission to change. The chaos of the moment might ignite goals or dreams—the drive to become something more, to do something more, to pursue things we didn't think we could.

Other times, the trigger to change is simply understanding the power of choice. We see opportunities and allow ourselves to pursue new and different things.

For app developer Lori Olson, the incentive was university. She needed a scholarship to finance her education, which meant she needed good marks. Lori had repeatedly been told she was too smart, so she deliberately hid, and even sabotaged, her brilliant mind. She kept a low profile with her grades to fit in with her schoolmates. With university on the horizon, that peer acceptance became less important than using her innate intelligence to get a scholarship. Lori stepped into her capabilities and showed up for success.

Longing creates momentum.

Marketing coach Kelsey Reidl, whose superpower is positivity, balances her sense of adventure with her approach to business. As an active outdoor person, Kelsey knows her plans can be interrupted by weather, accident, or circumstance. She gets a sense of satisfaction from handling those situations as they occur. It's probably not surprising she adapted this mindset to both her business and the entrepreneurs she helps with her Visionary Life program. "I love the sense of anticipation that happens when I approach life with the idea that adventure begins when something goes wrong . . . because things will definitely go wrong." Kelsey's attitude of adventure changes her perspectives and creates value.

One intriguing revelation from my chats with women was how often their crisis point came when they realized they had suppressed or abandoned some key parts of who they were. Once they reached a certain level of comfort in their lives, their longing to be who they were at their core was stronger than the need to fit in. They needed to feel they were being seen, heard, and recognized as individuals with a purpose.

Longing for purpose was often an inciting incident in their stories. While it wasn't always apparent at the time, longing often started women on a journey that transformed them. Speaking from experience, jewelry designer Anne-Marie Warburton says, "Sometimes the wrong train can take you to the right station."

So, what is it in our journeys that connects us to our core being? What inspires us to try new things and follow paths leading us to where we want to go?

I started to question if waiting for a crisis is necessary to break away from our limits. Can a sense of connection or intuition or destiny allow us to make different decisions, accept meaningful challenges, and own our lives? What inspires us to become who we *are* rather than who we are told we *should* be?

Most importantly, how long are we willing to wait before we show up and live fully?

A pause for thought before we leave this chapter:

Recall how trauma and trouble force us out of our comfort zones:

You've hit the ceiling.
Disruption triggers transformation.
Uncertainty invites an identity crisis.
Longing creates momentum.

10. MENTORS, MUSES, AND MOTHERS MODEL POSSIBILITIES.

My role model is the Future Me. I'm trying to learn from the best version of myself and model who I believe she is. –Kelsey Reidl

As women, we are influenced by how we see other women show up and behave. We model the women in our lives and the women we admire. When I asked women to name their mentors and role models, they named some famous women: Brené Brown, Glennon Doyle, Lisa Nichols, Oprah Winfrey.

I was intrigued that these role models were public figures, not individuals with whom the women had direct connection. Trailblazers and celebrities can inspire us, but who do we turn to for ongoing support and guidance as we contemplate our choices and identities?

In some cases, we turn to friends, siblings, and supportive communities for advice or guidance. We may admire the tact and kindness of a coworker or boss, or the way a friend can handle conflict without increasing tension. We may read biographies and memoirs hoping to learn secrets to success and happiness. But in the end, role models can't help us find our way if we don't relate to them.

Role models inspire us.

Julia Sen, the Possibility Psychologist, told me her earliest mentor was Fonzie, a character in the TV show *Happy Days*. While maybe not the typical TV star a young girl would idolize, Fonzie showed seven-year-old Julia anything was possible. He snapped his fingers and things magically happened. Watching this, Julia was infused with the belief that people had the power within themselves to create things.

"I fully understood that you don't just bang a jukebox and music starts, but it made me think, *Why not? I'm sure somebody could make that happen*. Even though it was a TV show, it impacted my whole view of life."

The idea of *Why Not?* shaped Julia's attitude and her choices. Her response to almost any situation was "Yes, I can." That attitude no doubt contributed to why Julia's family turned to her for answers when they had a problem or situation to address. Julia was the one who made things happen.

Julia had fictional Fonzie, and Cinderella had her Fairy Godmother. These magical beings created . . . well, magic. They made the impossible seem possible and inspired their protégées to make choices that led to possibilities.

Fairy Godmothers create magic.

When Cinderella decided to go to the ball, she and her tiny friends set to work with love and dedication to create a gown. Even when her evil stepmother destroyed her gown, Cinderella continued to believe she was worthy of showing up at the ball. That belief brought the Fairy Godmother to her aid. Cinderella helped manifest her future by doing the work to show up.

FAIRY GODMOTHER

Magic is...

a dollop of dreaming
+ a dash of daring
+ a cup of courage
↳ stirred with intention

Was Cinderella's Fairy Godmother a gift of her mindset? What if the real magic came from voices in her head telling her she was worthy of more?

For Sally Ng, the challenge wasn't a ball, but a birthday party. She wanted the perfect party for her twelfth birthday, and she wanted it at a new play arcade in the city. The party package was expensive and her immigrant parents couldn't afford it, but young Sally was determined. Her parents had shown her how to look at problems as challenges to be solved.

Sally found a possible solution when she discovered the arcade was having a talent show. The semi-final prize was a pizza and bowling party for ten people. The grand prize was a gymnastics party. Sally wanted to win not just one prize, but both. She immersed herself in the challenge, creating imaginative shows. And she achieved her goal—she won both prizes!

But that wasn't the end of the challenge. Like Cinderella, Sally needed transport to get to the ball: she had to get everyone across town to the venue. Sally didn't have a pumpkin, but she had gumption. She called her friends' parents and arranged drivers for everyone. She wasn't even twelve and Sally made the seemingly impossible happen.

How do the rest of us find the magic wand? Who teaches us about possibilities? Who teaches us about the magic that happens when we believe?

The reality is that our experiences are a result of our actions, and our actions are shaped by our choices. Which means that our Fairy Godmothers are a dollop of dreaming, a dash of daring, and a cup of courage, stirred with intention.

We can choose which voices and opinions to listen to, but we need to be intentional about it. When we blindly follow the expectations of others, we allow them to dictate our lives. When we give up our power of choice, we give up control.

At the same time, we can learn from others. People who guide us and encourage us to grow and move forward are our mentors and role models. They help us believe we are capable and deserving. They raise the Expectations Ceiling to a higher level of possibilities.

Some women consciously step into the role of role model and mentor. Mayor Dawn Arnold knew she would be held to high standards as the first female mayor of Moncton.

"Being in the spotlight means I can't screw up," she said. "I feel people are looking to me to be courageous, inspiring, and optimistic. I take the responsibility very, very seriously. I believe you can't be what you can't see. And by being a woman in leadership, I think it inspires young women to stand up and see what it looks like to be a woman leader."

Mothers model.

Many of the women who shared their stories with me were trailblazers who forged paths without guides to help them navigate the rough spots. In most cases, their mothers were their role models and biggest supporters. By pursuing degrees, careers, artistic talents, and self-expression, mothers showed daughters that owning their identity was not only doable, but it was also a priority. It meant hard work and sacrifice, but the rewards created a life worth celebrating.

Alex Cattoni's mother is one of those role models. She is a professor with a PhD in nursing who, at one point in time, was the single mother of two-year-old twins and a full-time grad student. She had to be tough to raise her kids, get multiple degrees, and achieve her dreams. She passed on this can-do mindset to Alex and modeled the message that being a girl didn't have to limit her. And it hasn't. Alex has succeeded in building a profitable and personally rewarding business in the Copy Posse.

Alicia Grayeb's Mexican mother taught her empathy and love, which radiate from Alicia. Even though her mother personally adhered to traditional roles, she wanted Alicia to be happy and express herself. Maintaining their own cultural connection didn't prevent Alicia's mother and father from freely supporting her when she moved across the ocean to embrace independence.

While Shirlee Sharkey credits her father with teaching her to be independent, it was her mother who taught her balance. An impulsive and playful woman, Shirlee's mother presented a creative side to counterbalance the discipline in Shirlee's life. This balance provided Shirlee with many of the tools she used to create a balanced culture at Saint Elisabeth Health (SE Health), a not-for-profit social enterprise focused on home care, seniors' lifestyle, and family caregiving.

Even traditional, stay-at-home mothers can give their daughters the gift of growing. Lori Olson's mother treated both her and her brother the same, telling them they could make their own choices. For Lori, that choice was an unconventional career path at the time: she was one of the first women to code software and quickly achieved status as a sought-after expert in app development.

When women talked about their mothers, the range of emotions they expressed underlined the power of a mother's influence. There were words of admiration and of resentment. Respect and disappointment. Some women trusted their mothers with their dreams and secrets, while others couldn't share their feelings for fear of rejection or discipline. In fact, some mothers were more like Cinderella's stepmother, fueling a sense of unworthiness that led to insecurity.

Still, these mothers were role models. Some were women their daughters wanted to emulate, and some became examples of who they didn't want to become.

Fathers expect.

Fathers of the women I talked to often played a different role in motivating them. Edye Hoffmann had an insightful perspective around the influence of fathers: "You want Dad to be proud of you. You know Mom will always love you, but Dad expects more of you."

Expects. That word says so much. Some of these fathers became role models to their daughters, but more often their biggest influence came from the expectations they placed on their children. Some daughters were expected to follow traditional careers and motherhood paths. Wanting more than what their parents had was considered uppity or selfish. Challenging tradition and norms risked being outcast.

The spoken and unspoken visions fathers had for their daughters (and their sons) set the tone for acceptance. Those lofty or limited expectations influenced their daughters' mindsets and choices. My own father, despite being strict about marriage and the Church, taught me to change the tires and oil in my car so I could be more independent.

Many women in business or entrepreneurship roles benefited from male role models. While finishing her studies, Veronica Piacek worked with her father in his business, absorbing his work ethic and the value of relationships. She credits these early experiences with her tendency to fight for what she believes in. Not surprisingly, the male managers she appreciated the most reminded her of her dad. Their values aligned with hers, and she trusted them to help her achieve her goals.

Sadly, some of the women Veronica worked with didn't support her career success. A few even tried to sabotage her by undermining her efforts. This type of subterfuge isn't uncommon as women step into increasingly more responsible and powerful roles.

Jo Gillibrand has often seen this dynamic enfold through her coaching and training roles. She suggests some women have a strange relationship with power because power is currently defined by a macho and capitalist culture. A few of the maladapted responses she's noticed through her work include impostor syndrome, detachment, and even bullying.

Sharon Preszler was more fortunate because she found role models and mentors through two groups of women who share her love for flying. The Women's Air Service Pilots (WASPS) is a group of adventurous women who became pilots during the Second World War. They may not have flown in battle, but the very fact these young women learned to fly, taught men how to fly, and transported planes and people across the USA in the 1940s is an inspiration to future women pilots. The second organization, the Chick Fighter Pilot Association (CFPA), has a narrower focus, but Sharon says the women in both these organizations help and support each other without backstabbing.

Why can't we find more women role models like this? There are many anecdotes about how women have trouble supporting other women. Instead of friendly competition, a component of envy can kick in, which some theories tie back to our survival instincts. Eliminating female competition created better opportunities for choosing mates who could provide security, or even privilege.

Defensiveness and envy might also result from a sense of scarcity. When women—or for that matter, minorities or marginalized individuals—have fought hard to get to where they are, they may get protective. They may not want to lose what they have achieved. Perhaps that's why we hear about someone who finally *made it* figuratively pushing the ladder away so that others can't follow in her footsteps. She doesn't want competition. She doesn't want to risk falling backward.

The Dementia Lady, Edye Hoffmann, has seen this resistance firsthand. She loves working with people who have different strengths because she believes she can learn from them. She sees the difference in personalities as an asset, but not all the people she's approached share her perspective. Edye has been told she's strong and confident enough and she doesn't need help. As a result, some women won't support her. Then there are those who are intimidated by her confidence and avoid her. Either way, they don't support Edye in achieving her goals, which makes it challenging for Edye to support them.

What happens when talented and ambitious women can't find role models? Some of them create their own.

Kelsey Reidl, who has a successful marketing consulting business, says her mother set the tone for Kelsey to explore possibilities. "She thought outside the box and just didn't care what people thought of her."

Kelsey appreciated her mother's rebellious nature and set out to explore how she could show up just as strong. She listened to thought leaders, experts, and other people when something about them appealed to who she wanted to become. She used this insight to create a model for Future Kelsey, which she called "The best version of myself."

Shirlee Sharkey, the retired CEO of SE Health, also learned from observation. She deliberately studied others, watching how they made decisions and worked with people. Doing so taught her both who she wanted to emulate and who she didn't want to imitate. In this way, she created her own mind-mentor, Future Shirlee. She told herself: "This is the woman I want to be like."

Today, social media provides us with an endless scroll of potential role models. The key is finding people we trust . . . people we can relate to and learn from, rather than just envy. As a result, we're changing the traditional definition of a role model. It isn't just age or experience that can help us grow, it is shared experiences and goals.

Mentors and muses share.

Stephanie Major, the woman who once hated herself for wanting more, now focuses on *intentional living*. One of her mentors is her friend Rebecca, whom she considers a peer and soul sister. "We mentor each other. We practice receiving and allowing one another to love and receive that love." By allowing themselves to be vulnerable and by sharing proud moments with each other, these friends discovered how to surrender the need for perfection and fully step into themselves.

Once we get past the fear of rejection, we can see there is magic in sharing. How do we learn the secret? How do we find women we can trust to become role models or mentors?

One of our best options is to seek others who are further along the paths we are on. People who are growth-oriented are comfortable with other people's success. They are better listeners and tend to be team players. They want to help solve issues. But alignment is important.

Contemporary artist, humanitarian, and author Patricia Gagic is generous with her time and loves to connect people. She believes the best mentor to guide you is the person who has mastered what you are dreaming you could do. Finding such a mentor means being clear on what you are looking for, even if you don't know what the outcome will be. It also means being open to learning rather than seeking someone who will simply agree with you.

Patricia says, "If you ask me for help, and I agree to take on the responsibility, I have to figure out how to help you. If I suggest something, and you say, 'Not interested,' I may not be the right mentor for you. I may want to help, but you may not be open to learning because you're just trying to find a way of validating your decisions.

We need to be open if we want to learn from our role models and mentors. After all, we look for role models because we want to see who we could be if we allowed ourselves to evolve and grow. Our search for these guides means being open to exploring who we are and how we can evolve into more.

A pause for thought before we leave this chapter:

> **Recall how mentors, muses, and mothers model possibilities:**
>
> Role models inspire us.
> Fairy Godmothers create magic.
> Mothers model. Fathers expect.
> Mentors and muses share.

11. IDENTITY BECOMES A JOURNEY.

You do not have to change who you are.
You only have to become more of who you are, at your best.
–Sally Hogshead

We read about identity. We talk about identity. We spend endless hours wondering about identity, asking ourselves: *Who am I? How do I find my Self?*

We agonize over why we are who we are. Whether we like who we are. Why we don't like who we are. Who we'd like to be. Who we think we could be. Who others want us to be. Who we dream of becoming.

Maybe we're asking the wrong question. *Who am I?* creates the impression that we have a single identity, as if who we are is fixed and rigid. Is that why we hesitate to own our identity? It sounds permanent. Perhaps that's why we avoid risk and play small—because it's safer than tackling the unknown.

What if we didn't have to find ourselves? What if we changed one word in that intimidating sentence? How would we feel if we changed *find* to *become*?

How do I become my Self?

Being is the first step to becoming.

Our thought processes shift when we abandon the idea of finding ourselves and instead focus on *being* and *becoming* ourselves. When we allow ourselves to *be* and to develop, we give ourselves permission to experience life at its fullest rather than seeking specific, finite endpoints. We can evolve and still be true to who we are.

Artist and author Patricia Gagic believes the journey to our best selves starts with being aware of who we are, where we belong, and what we seek. She speaks from experience. From the time she was young, Patricia had an inner belief she could be whatever she wanted to be. She knew she wanted to master her art, and she set out to turn that vision into reality.

It wasn't easy. As she explained, her life journey was challenging and complicated. "On multiple occasions throughout life, I had to stand up and make an instant decision about whether I would collapse or survive. I had so many things happen to me, I didn't have time for a pity party. I had to pick up and move on."

Move on, she did. Patricia dedicated time, effort, and energy into becoming an exceptionally well-rounded woman. She became a bank manager by the time she was twenty-five years old. Then she apprenticed with the great French artist Master "Dragan Dragic" for over twenty-five years. She also married and had a family.

Patricia's vision kept her moving forward through these experiences. Her childhood taught her to be resilient, and it also fueled her curiosity. She had absorbed the energies in her environments and started questioning why people attached themselves to suffering. While she knew she would not choose to carry so much emotional baggage, she wanted to understand the source of suffering.

As a seeker, Patricia sought knowledge and expertise in everything she did. She immersed herself in discovery for decades, studying meditation, traditions, philosophies, and religions, constantly digging deep into the power of awareness, the flow of karma, and the motivation surrounding choices.

Her experiences taught Patricia that awareness and confidence are linked. She says, "We create the capacity to find our best self when we are aware of who we are, make intentional choices, and design a path for ourselves. When we are aware we have choice, we can give ourselves permission to take action, to immerse ourselves in moments, and to experience them fully. Practicing action is key to achieving mastery, and confidence comes with mastery."

It's apparent that Patricia's choices, mindset, and actions shaped her into who she is today—a disciplined, determined, and creative woman who shows up with heart. She is not only an artist, successful entrepreneur, and businesswoman, but she is also a compassionate humanitarian who built a library and supported schools in Cambodia.

Patricia's art reflects her mastery of both the craft and emotion of creation. She is one of the Top 10 Contemporary Artists in the world, with her work showcased in the Louvre and the Vatican, as well as in homes and galleries all over the world.

Yet success hasn't changed Patricia's core belief in karma and being of service to the world. She makes time to show up as a role model and mentor, working to raise the bar for others. Her gifts to the world are generous and multidimensional.

Shirlee Sharkey is another woman who was always driven. She loved challenges. She loved puzzles. Growing up, she was determined to create a life where she could solve problems and become an influence. And she made it happen.

"If there were problems, I was helping to solve them, and probably taking the lead. I am impatient with waiting around, so I'll take the lead and work with everyone to find a solution."

Although it sounds like Shirlee wants control, her approach is not about being *right* but about finding the best solution. She takes the lead to make things happen, not because she wants to be the expert. One of her assets is having the confidence to say, "I don't know this stuff."

Many women feel uncomfortable taking the lead without knowing everything and having each and every one of the competencies needed. Shirlee takes a different approach, citing sports as a source of confidence in her leadership approach.

"Teams have all these players who bring incredible strengths. You need to figure out who is really good where, and who to put on the front line. I was usually a captain because, while I was not great with anything, I could make decisions and set up the team to perform. And it also meant I had to be okay with practice, disappointment, and the lack of success."

Bringing sports principles into her life allowed Shirlee to build confidence in her leadership. When something didn't work, she wanted to know why. Her perspective is that there's a reason for everything, and she will find out what it is in time. Lack of success does not mean quitting; it means assessing.

Shirlee believes impact comes from combining our values with action. This philosophy guided her career and life choices, leading her to Saint Elisabeth Health (SE Health), where she recently retired as

CEO after thirty years. Shirlee's leadership style helped her attract a great team and continue to find solutions. This combination built SE Health into a leading social enterprise and one of the largest diversified home health organizations in Canada.

She credits her own growth within the organization to an environment that allowed her to be bold and innovative, but it was her vision and drive that created an organization in alignment with her values. Shirlee's confidence in her vision made it happen.

Dreaming changes us.

Tammy Price makes incredible pastries. More importantly, she shares them. Baking is one of her love languages, providing both expression and release for Tammy.

The complexity of love, and love languages, has been a theme in Tammy's journey. From a young age, she's known she wanted to own who she is, but it was not an easy or straightforward path. Her family had conservative and traditional lives and expected her to fall into line.

But Tammy wanted more out of life. Her desire to own her identity and her future made her feel like the black sheep of the family. Tammy doesn't object to that description, though. She doesn't define a black sheep as a rebel but as an individual with different dreams and ambitions from her family. To Tammy, staying safe and doing what her parents expected was giving away her choice and her life. It meant abandoning herself, and she couldn't do that.

Tammy had dreams to follow. Those dreams lingered in her thoughts and eventually led her to study the roots of abandonment and rejection. Insight she gained from those studies—and from leaving her marriage—helped Tammy find a sense of balance. The knowledge and skills she learned also helped Tammy navigate the physical and emotional pain she experienced when she fought her personal battle with cancer at the same time she watched her mother lose her fight to cancer.

Tammy's desire to find a better life ultimately led her to become a medical intuitive. By choosing to follow her feelings and doing what felt right for her, Tammy gave herself permission to grow. She now uses her innate skills to help others heal.

Being the black sheep of the family is definitely a recurring theme. Many women are willing to defy family and cultural expectations to become who they feel they need to be. In one sense, being a black sheep allows us to reject limits and believe in ourselves.

When we believe in ourselves and allow ourselves to *be* more, we change the thoughts and words that dictate our mindset. We change the choices we make, the options we see, and who we can become.

A JOURNEY OF DISCOVERY

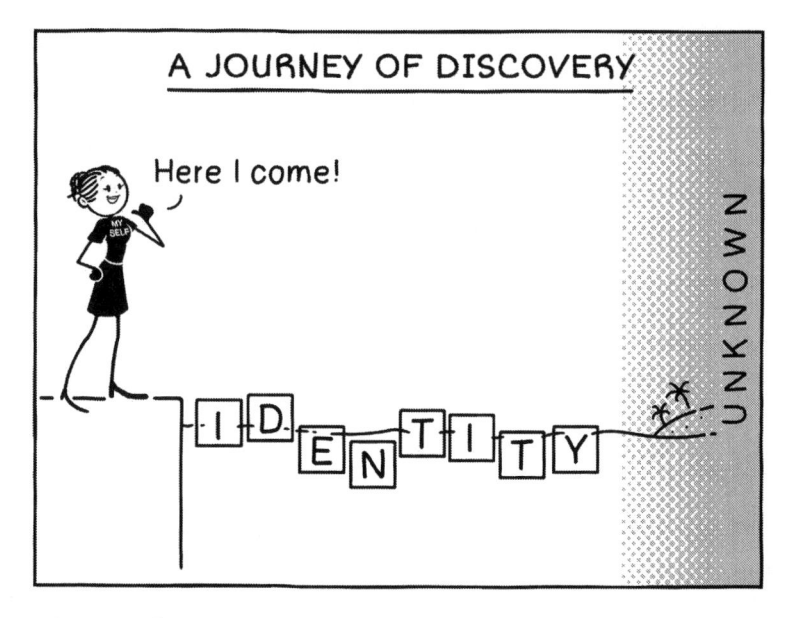

Here I come!

[Illustration: A figure labeled "MYSELF" stands on a cliff facing stepping stones spelling "IDENTITY" leading across to an island labeled "UNKNOWN"]

Leaving is a beginning.

Being able to push boundaries allows us to let go of what is no longer serving us. I once introduced myself to a group as an ex-accountant, ex-analyst, ex-Calgarian, ex-wife, ex-advertising executive, and ex-Torontonian. Some people may interpret discarding these identities as evidence I couldn't commit, or possibly that I wasn't able to succeed in these roles. I see it differently.

I see leaving behind things from my past as stepping stones to my present. I had to let go of who I was in those roles and places in order to step into who I became next. I also know who I am today will be a stepping stone to who Future Vera becomes. Growth comes when we take steps. We can't cross the river if we don't move from one stepping stone to the next.

Sometimes what gives us courage to take the next step is realizing there is a reason to cross. Opportunities and options are waiting for us to discover them. And even though we may not think we have the skills to do certain things, if we want them badly enough, we learn how. We find ways because we can see possibilities and rewards.

What if we believed there were no ceilings to the possibilities in our lives? What if the Glass Ceiling and the Expectations Ceiling crumbled when we challenged biases and boundaries? What would happen if we stepped outside the box and gave ourselves permission to show up the way we want to?

Here's the thing—we can. We can change our thoughts, our expectations, and our actions. We can do more, be more, and achieve more.

Identity evolves.

We don't have to change who we are; we need to *show up* as who we are. The way to become limitless is by becoming more of who we are. The process is a journey of discovery. We grow, we change, we see things differently.

When we discard the idea that identity is an endpoint and view it as an evolution, we create unlimited possibilities for ourselves. We can be whoever we want to be at any point in time. We're not finished being or learning who we are until the very end of our lives.

A pause for thought before we leave this chapter:

> **Recall how identity becomes a journey:**
> ___
>
> Being is the first step to becoming.
> Dreaming changes us.
> Leaving is a beginning.
> Identity evolves.

12. INTENTIONAL CHOICES SHAPE OUR FUTURE.

Always be a leader, even if you're only leading yourself.
—Jennifer Minella

Identity is complex. It forms and changes as we learn and grow, falter and fall. It morphs as we find our footing and try to fit into family and community. And because safety is important, we may camouflage our public identity to protect ourselves from anticipated threats and destruction.

Why? Because identity is emotionally linked to feelings of belonging. Identity reflects who we are in any environment. It connects us to family, friends, and communities. Those links can feel fragile, which means that our need to belong exerts an element of emotional pressure on our choices.

We might become chameleons to blend in with certain communities or groups. Blending in may create security, but it also leaves us in conflict. How can we find out who we truly are when we're constantly changing to be accepted by others? We can lose our sense of individual identity by focusing on fitting in.

Our skills, experiences, and strengths are integral to who we are. They intersect with our actions, behaviors, and choices—the ABCs that line the paths of our lives and create our identity. Those ABCs are influenced by the need to belong. Following the need to belong is almost like following breadcrumbs others placed on the paths in front of us.

Breadcrumbs lead us astray.

The crumbs we pick up lead us in the direction others want us to go. They lure us away from our dreams and distract us from exploring the beauty awaiting us just off the beaten path.

Going where we are expected to go can be a trap. When we don't choose for ourselves, we don't get to know ourselves. This lack of knowledge prevents us from fully embracing who we are and being ourselves. When we let other people define us, their need for conformity confines us.

Before we can intentionally create our own identity, we need to get off the beaten path. We need to step outside the boxes we've been put into. Maybe that's why we need to let go of so much of who we *think* we are to find out who we *actually* are.

One of the hardest things to let go of is an identity that no longer serves us. The founder of We Wild Women, Renée Warren, believes human beings are supposed to evolve and change and our identity changes at the same time. "What I do isn't who I am, and who I am isn't what I do," she says. "What you do changes in your lifetime. Who you are is your essence. It's okay to go through transitions because who we are at our core is always going to be the same."

Coach and trainer Jo Gillibrand calls this metamorphosis a series of mini reinventions. Her career path has spanned the arts, training, coaching, and building communities. Sometimes these transitions were thrust upon her, like when she took on the role of trainer for an arts organization because there was no one else to do it. Other times she's taken chances and deliberately reached for opportunities.

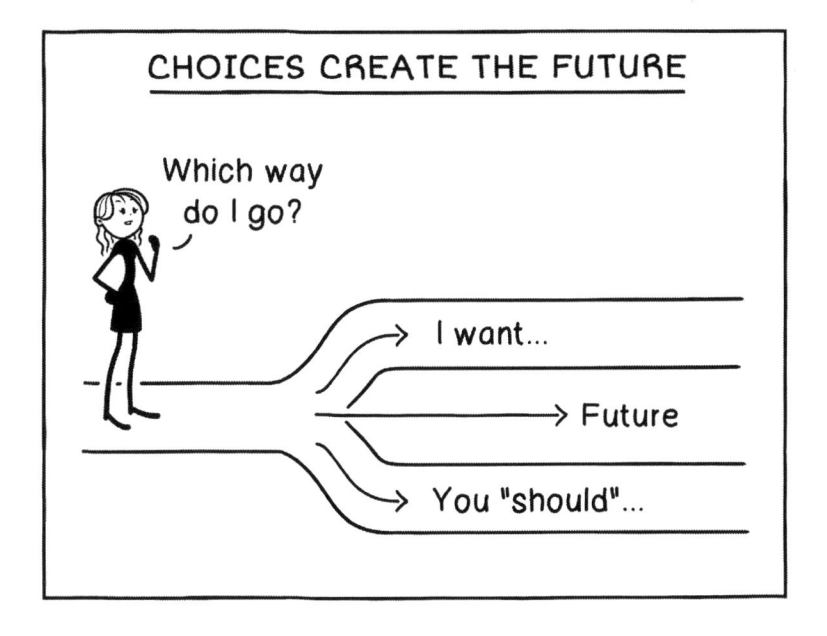

CHOICES CREATE THE FUTURE

Which way do I go?

→ I want...

→ Future

→ You "should"...

Purpose is important to embracing our best selves. Edye Hoffmann expresses it this way: "I have a drive to get out of bed and produce something that lets me hold my head up high. I love the feeling of making an impact . . . making a difference. I'm not going to stop doing that."

How do we decide what we do and how we show up in our lives? We access the power of choice.

We can choose our own paths.

I love trails that weave through forests and follow streams. Sometimes I follow marked paths, and other times I find myself wandering aimlessly. When I come to a fork, I have to choose which way to go. If I've never been on either of the trails before, and if I don't have a map or a compass to guide me, I make a decision based on what I know. Is the path uphill or downhill? Is it going generally in the direction I want to go? Am I considering a circuitous route because it looks easier? How much effort will be involved taking one versus the other? What about the views? What do I think I will see and experience in one direction versus the other?

When I'm walking with others, I must also consider their perspectives. Am I making a choice for myself, or one based on what others in the group want? Am I relying on their knowledge and capabilities, or am I falling in line with their fears? Is it time to be a leader, a follower, or a voice of reason? Sometimes dissention is the best way to find the right track.

Every decision I make, every step I take, is a step toward my future. As soon as I take that step, I am in my future. I can turn around, look back, and say, "I took a step toward a future I don't want." At that point I have the ability to circle back to where I really want to go. It's about making the right decision for where I am at in any moment in time.

What do others do when they face decisions? The answer I got when I asked women this question was consistent: *feel the answer.*

Don't think—feel.

Alicia Grayeb takes time to research and explore her options for big decisions, but in the end, she always circles back to what feels right, especially if the options present similar opportunities. Her confidence in her instincts is grounded in positive experiences. She never regretted her decision to leave Mexico nor her more recent choice of Canada for her home.

As a medical intuitive, Tammy Price knows the power of the body to sense alignment. She uses feelings as her guiding light and helps others access their body knowledge to get, and stay, healthy.

Anne-Marie Warburton learned to trust her intuition. The owner of Gallery Gemma Jewellery doesn't bother with pro-versus-con lists because she discovered asking questions is one of her greatest gifts.

Besides, her years of experience proved that her intuition has always been right.

Balancing logic and intuition seems to be the most common approach to making decisions. Even women who make pro-and-con lists talked about how emotional responses were often the deciding factor in making choices.

After that, the most important step is taking action. Marketing guru Veronica Piacek talks about the danger of limbo. "It paralyzes. It prevents you from moving forward. If you do a pro-and-con list and can't figure it out, go with your gut."

Gut, instinct, intuition, feelings—these are the heart center for many important decisions. Copy Posse boss Alex Cattoni ensures her decisions are in alignment with her values by testing how each decision feels. For her, that alignment means knowing she's growing, having fun, and helping people at the same time.

Renée Warren not only embraces the power of choice, but she teaches people in her programs how to make decisions. She calls it the *Head, Heart and Gut* approach, and she uses this exercise to teach women to make decisions based on what they want to do, not what's expected of them.

Using a slightly different approach, Koffee Beauty founder Estelle Doiron starts her decision-making analysis by figuring out what she needs to learn. It's a habit she picked up from a life filled with sports.

I loved the way she explained it: "If you take the basics of sports, you need to learn a skill, and to learn a skill, you need to practice. The more you practice, the better you get. Once you're in the game, if you do what you practiced and you practiced enough, you will do well. It's the same in business. At first you don't know what you're doing. You need to find out what you need to learn and how to practice doing it."

The importance of practice frequently came up. Women who had played sports learned the value of trying, failing, and knowing that failure was actually part of the trial-and-error process—a way of learning something new. Sports wasn't the only route to this learning, however. Mayor Dawn Arnold got the same benefit from band practice. Almost any activity can create a mindset of continual learning and growth when it establishes the discipline of paying attention to what we're doing.

Cathy Sweet called it *the practice of making mistakes*. She told me: "I think the only way to gain confidence is through experience. The key word is *gain*. It doesn't just happen. You can read lots of books, but you grow in situations that force you to be confident. You must allow and invite those situations. Do uncomfortable things so that when you have no choice, you know you can show up with confidence."

These situations could be facing the discomfort of making sales calls, negotiating, creating social media posts, presenting workshops, or even speaking up to support others. The more we step into courage and confidence, the more we can expect to achieve.

The secret ingredient to changing expectations is intentional choice. When we believe we have the power to choose and to change, we create possibilities for growth.

Attention follows intention.

Dr. Joe Dispenza says where we place our attention is where we place our energy, and where we place our energy, we expand. If our attention follows our thoughts, it prompts the question: Are we focusing on possibilities or limits?

My father gave similar advice when he was teaching me to drive. He told me to keep my eyes on the road if I started to lose control. He said we usually end up going in the direction we focus on, so if I paid attention to the road, not the ditch, I would stay on the road.

All this is sound and obvious advice, yet how often do we pay more attention to what we fear than where we want to go?

Stephanie Major introduced me to the phrase "perfectly imperfect." It's about accepting wherever we are in the moment. She says, "Instead of trying to always get there, I accept that I am already there. Does that mean I still want to grow and evolve? Absolutely. I can still want more, but I consider myself whole. It's who I am in the moment—perfectly imperfect."

As artist Patricia Gagic said, "We own our identity when we no longer need others to feel complete."

A pause for thought before we leave this chapter:

> ### Recall how intentional choices shape our futures:
>
> Breadcrumbs lead us astray.
> We can choose our own paths.
> Don't think—feel.
> Attention follows intention.

PART 4:

What does success look like?

> SUCCESS IS A PRIVILEGE.
> IT GIVES YOU THE POWER TO CHOOSE. —SALLY NG

Patience pays off.

I waited for my bosses to say no.

I was presenting recommendations for a new account director, fully expecting the most qualified candidate would be rejected because his salary ask was significantly above the range we'd advertised.

We were looking for someone with specific experience to handle a big account for the advertising agency. The most qualified individual was a very confident young man who wanted a salary considerably higher than what we were paying our other—female—account directors.

I was making $40,000 as director of Client Services. I couldn't imagine the general manager and creative director approving $55,000 (which is about $132K in today's dollars) for someone reporting to me. But when they looked at the résumé and the salary request, they didn't hesitate.

They told me to hire him.

I was too shocked to speak. I had just learned how little women were valued. How little I was valued. Despite everything I'd done to turn the organization around, despite my track record for increasing profitability and client satisfaction, my bosses were willing to pay almost 40 percent more for a man than they were for me, his female manager!

I walked out of the room and sent the offer.

I cried that night and almost every night for a week. Not only did I feel underappreciated, but I felt used. I hated myself for not speaking up. I hated this cocky upstart who was valued more than I was. I started looking for another job.

Over drinks one night, I told a friend how I was feeling, expecting her to console me. She didn't. She told me to stop allowing myself to be a victim. That wasn't what I had expected her to say.

However, she didn't shake me up and then leave me hanging. She challenged me to take a different perspective on the situation and look for possible resolutions. Importantly, she told me to put myself in management's shoes and find a solution that would allow them to save face when the discrepancy was highlighted.

I knew complaining to the general manager wasn't the right approach because he didn't like conflict. He also wouldn't want to be called out for bias in hiring and compensation. I needed to find the right time, place, and message to stand up for myself, and maybe even change the agency's sliding scale for female employees.

The new hire turned out to be a good account director. He impressed the client and management, which made me look good, even though my frustration with the situation continued to fester. But, thanks to my girlfriend, I had a plan.

Three months later, when we were doing annual salary reviews, I presented a list of recommendations for generous staff increases. Because profits were up, the increases were all approved. Mine was the last name on the list.

The creative director looked at me with a big smile and said I'd been doing great work. "You deserve a nice increase. What do you think would be appropriate?"

My heart skipped. This was my opportunity.

"As long as I'm making more than anyone reporting to me, I'll be happy with whatever you give me."

"Of course," he replied. I watched his face as he studied the salary sheet and realized the implications of what he had just agreed to. There was no backing down.

I was rewarded for standing up for myself that day. I received a 60 percent increase in pay.

13. SUCCESS IS AN EMOTION.

Success becomes any tender moment, big or small, where you feel fulfilled. –Shirlee Sharkey

---

We live in a world that defines success in terms of money, possessions, power, and prestige. Yet when I asked women for their definitions of success, without hesitation every one of them gave me an answer involving emotion.

Instead of telling me they wanted to be millionaires or billionaires, or to grow their companies 10x, or to buy a mansion on an island, or to have a certain title, they told me what success *feels* like.

Success is a feeling.
Success is moments.
Success is happiness.
Success is contentment.
Success is knowing I don't have to be driven.
Success is feeling free to be me.
Success is balance.

Success is letting go.
Success is love.
Success is stepping into the sunshine and breathing the air every morning.
Success is being alive.

The most inspiring aspect of these answers is the way they highlight how success is achievable every day. These women have built companies and schools for children. They have created safe spaces for people to heal, developed programs to help others live their dreams, and helped parents raise their children with resilience and love. They have championed literacy, sustainability, and community involvement. They've traveled to gain experience and share cultures. They have written books, won awards, and shared their art with the world. They've achieved financial success, world recognition, prestige, and accolades.

Despite all these accomplishments, they all said true success comes from within.

Our definitions of success may vary, but we know how it feels. We know when our hearts sing, and we know the awe we feel when we can sit for a moment and say, "I did it." We feel successful when we look at children, women, disadvantaged individuals, or others whose lives we transformed—including our own.

```
┌─────────────────────────────────────────┐
│            SUCCESS IS...                │
│                                         │
│   Freedom              Balance          │
│                                         │
│   Happiness            Love             │
│                                         │
│   Contentment          Letting go       │
│                                         │
│      Choice           Moments           │
│                                         │
│          Being fully alive              │
└─────────────────────────────────────────┘
```

Success is personal.

If we embrace the idea of success as a personal and emotional experience, we can celebrate every time we make a choice that brings us closer to achieving our dreams and living our values. We can bask in the knowledge we are creating our best lives by being true to who we are, while making a difference in our worlds.

Shirlee Sharkey, the recently retired CEO of SE Health, has a string of accomplishments she achieved over her career, yet her definition of success is not focused on outer recognition. She advocates viewing success from the perspective of impact: "Live with your heart, because then the results go beyond a personal level. Success becomes any tender moment, big or small, where you feel fulfilled. It doesn't really matter what it is. Sometimes it's a big, quantifiable goal, but it could be a wonderful conversation or an accomplishment—anything from working out, to healthy eating, to staying intentional and focused."

Success does not have to be quiet, but neither does it have to be loud. Rather than associate success with money or achievements, many of these women measured it in terms of moving forward—letting go, grieving, growing, and freeing themselves to be all they could be. They embraced consciously living today as a way to create the best opportunities for their future, and in the process, reaching a state of being that Edye Hoffmann called "future-oriented presence."

It's such a logical and rewarding approach to life, yet we aren't taught to see success in the present moment. Too often we spend time looking back to track success or racing ahead to find the next elusive target. The irony is, living in each moment and creating memories of those moments is what brings a sense of joy and success to many of us. Little moments create satisfaction, and layers of those satisfying moments build into lasting feelings of achievement over time.

In her early years, jewelry designer Anne-Marie Warburton had a different point of view: "I used to say success was making $1 million. Now I feel it's living a joyful life—one full of balance, good health, good relationships, good spiritual life, community, friendships with incredible women, and the work I love."

When software developer Lori Olson talks about success, her strong work ethic and analytical mind are evident. She's a perfectionist who sets the bar for herself as high as possible. "Good enough isn't enough for me. Never has been, never will be." Lori has achieved recognition and acclaim as an app developer, trainer, and expert in her field. She's grateful for the recognition, but her pride in her work is what drives her. She validates herself and calls anyone else's opinion "icing on the cake."

Sharon Preszler is proud of what she has achieved as a fighter pilot, mother, and motivational speaker. She believes these successes add to her happiness, but her emotional contentment comes from how she chooses to live. Sharon doesn't have a bucket list. She's not waiting for experiences in the future . . . because she's happy with life as it is. She knows she is fortunate to do what she has done, and she believes she can choose to create more opportunities and possibilities in the future. One of her mantras is: "Follow your dreams and don't let other people's judgment stop you."

Veronica Piacek echoed the importance of family in achieving a fulfilling life. One of her greatest satisfactions comes from knowing she never missed an important event with her two girls while she built her career in marketing. It was a deliberate choice. Veronica knew she wanted control of her life, so she focused her attention on what mattered the most to her: family.

Her advice is surprisingly simple: "Don't be afraid to say *no*. It's the fastest route to *yes*."

Success is not dependent on being a good student, either. Both Renée Warren and Melissa Duguay were C students. Neither one did very well in school; however, they were the girls other people gravitated toward. They were fun, positive, and energetic. Melissa and Renée may not have been school smart, but they were people smart. They both channeled their skill sets into successful careers and businesses—Melissa as a renowned hairstylist and sought-after platform artist who helps women look and feel amazing, and Renée as a successful entrepreneur who helps women achieve their dreams.

Success is alignment.

One intriguing aspect of these women's definitions of success is the way they differ from traditional measures: the acquisition of power, possessions, and prestige. All three attributes fall within the lower levels on Maslow's Hierarchy—within the *deficiency needs*. The way women described success tended toward the top of the pyramid, where the *being needs* reside. In other words, women tend to see emotional fulfillment as their goal rather than financial or status gains. That's not to say men don't seek fulfillment, but it seems women may not need to acquire traditional trappings of success enroute to fulfillment.

Which doesn't mean women can't have both. Alex Cattoni has a thriving business, but she considers the traditional definition of success in terms of dollars as a type of competition for recognition, not true fulfillment.

As an overachiever, Alex has a strong narrative of success, but her goals extend beyond revenue. She doesn't measure success based on her bank account or billings. She wants to help more people while having more fun, and she believes this mindset will ultimately lead to financial gain. Consequently, Alex tries her best to measure her achievements on how far she's come versus how far she wants to go. She believes we risk feeling constantly inadequate if we're always comparing our success against an ever-moving horizon, worrying about how to earn more and grow more than last year.

To create her version of success, Alex focuses on what kind of life she wants and what business model will support that life. It's a model that works for others, too. She often asks her clients to think about building their businesses with fulfillment in mind: "What do you really want? Where is the balance? Create the life you actually want."

Recognizing and celebrating success helps Alex take more risks, gain more experience, and hone her skills so she can continue to grow. She notes that confidence comes from acting with courage. When she does, and she's in full alignment doing what she wants to do, she's happy and content.

Success is freedom.

Freedom consistently came up during discussions around success. What freedom means varied, but it generally came down to having the freedom of choice. In some cases, it was freedom to travel. For others, it was freedom to spend time with family, to flex the day, or to change direction at will. Often, freedom simply meant not to have to answer to anyone else.

Freedom may have many forms, but the definitions I heard typically centered around feelings like excitement, anticipation, reward, contribution, and love. Freedom gives us access to creativity, artistry, nature, love, giving, healing, and leaving a legacy of helping others.

The power of permission to want more and be more is a gift we give ourselves. Without giving ourselves permission to *be*, we hide our gifts, we play small, or we wait for perfection. The world doesn't get a chance to see how beautiful we are, and we don't get a chance to become all we have the potential to be.

"If you're lucky enough in life to come to a point where you realize, *This is why I'm here*, you've found one half of success," says Stephanie Major, who has embraced intentional living as her mantra. Taking action on purpose contributes to our feelings of success.

Success comes from within.

Success isn't reliant on breaking through the Glass Ceiling. That's an external interpretation. The internal view of success is knowing we can set our expectations higher than any ceiling and then step into the person we need to be to achieve our own expectations and meet our own goals. To stretch, grow, and become more.

In this sense, success is becoming more of who we are at our core by celebrating and sharing our gifts. Success is knowing we deserve what we receive and knowing we can help others achieve and grow as well.

Psychologist Julia Sen sees it as an evolution: "As long as you're trying to learn new things, you're growing, and growing is what success is about. It's the energy of feeling alive doing whatever you're doing."

Mindfulness coach Jo Gillibrand has a similar point of view, calling success the right balance of work, life, and spiritual growth, which can lead to a sense of achievement and pride in yourself as a person.

Of note, success isn't found in a bank balance. Knowing the money is there to do what we dream of doing is welcomed, but money itself is only a tool to help us achieve our dreams and goals. Our relationships matter. Family matters. So do children and friends and animals. Nature, beauty, and living fully all matter. Doing meaningful work matters.

We matter too. We are here to change the course of lives. Maybe one life. Maybe dozens. Maybe thousands or millions. Success is knowing we make a difference.

A pause for thought before we leave this chapter:

> **Here's why success is an emotion:**
>
> Success is personal.
> Success is alignment.
> Success is freedom.
> Success comes from within.

14. SUCCESS IS BELIEVING.

I don't need a bucket list. My life is rounded. I'm happy with who I am and where I'm at. –Sharon Preszler

---

If we embrace the concept that success comes from within, our thoughts become the parameters dictating what we believe we can achieve with our lives. The way we talk to and about ourselves shapes not only our mindset, but also our identity. We show up confident when we are being true to ourselves.

Do the words you use to think about and describe yourself create the image of who you want to be, or how you want to be seen?

We become our thoughts.

When I visit my friend Jeannie, she's usually hanging around home in her department store jeans. She knows they're starting to sag in the butt, but they're comfortable. Besides, it's just her friends who see her wearing them, and we're usually dressed casually too.

When we go out, however, Jeannie puts on her designer jeans. She's a different person in those jeans. She seems to stand taller. She holds her shoulders back and her head up. She shows up with more confidence, and people are attracted to her uplifting energy.

Not long ago we were chatting about the future, and Jeannie slumped in her chair. She stared into her coffee for a bit and then admitted she didn't know how long she would have a career.

"Sales is so competitive, and younger people are way better with social media and new technology. I'm too old. I don't know if I can do this anymore."

It struck me that Jeannie's opinion of herself was starting to sag in the butt. Her confidence was being eroded by the voices in her head, not by her capabilities. She needed to challenge her damaging thought patterns and I had an idea how to start.

"Go upstairs and put on your designer jeans. Then come back down, and we're going to find the words that flatter you as much as those jeans do."

And we did.

Jeannie has superpowers, so we named them. She's a *skilled negotiator*, an *incredible relationship builder*, and an *innate problem-solver*. Those skills cultivate long-term client retention and open the door for incremental business. Jeannie's contribution to a company's bottom line is compound growth. She brings solid value to a company . . . in fact, she is the perfect salesperson!

Jeannie sat taller when we listed her strengths. These new labels were like her designer jeans—they created an image she was proud to wear. The right *wordz* allowed Jeannie to walk into the world and back to work with a whole new perspective around who she is and what she can do.

As mentioned in the introduction, I spell wordz with a zed (a zee) when they are *intentional* and empowering. The unusual spelling disrupts the brain's complacency. It interrupts the subconscious loop of beliefs running amuck in our heads and challenges us to think. To ask *why*.

That's the point. We hack our mindsets by disrupting thought patterns, which causes our brains to pause and re-evaluate assumptions about what we can do.

If Jeannie had continued to think and say she was too old, her self-image would deteriorate. She wouldn't show up with confidence. Her performance would reflect her limiting thoughts, and she would become the poor salesperson she had started telling herself she was.

Accurate and empowering wordz allowed Jeannie to let go of limiting beliefs about her age and capabilities. They gave her permission to own her gifts and show up with presence and confidence. She owned her identity as a superb salesperson. That's the power of wordz.

We show up with confidence.

Just like clothing labels, word labels create images of who we are and give us a sense of where we belong. When we intentionally choose wordz that reflect how we want to be seen, we change how we show up . . . and the presence and energy we project changes how other people see us.

Whether we realize it or not, we get put into boxes, and those boxes have labels telling others who we are. Sorry, but it's true. Our identities are defined by how other people label us, as well as how we label ourselves.

We amplify external influences on our identity when we align with the visible imagery of brands. It's an easy trap to fall into. Brand marketing uses art and science to create images—auras—that people relate to. But most marketers are more concerned with us fitting into *their* boxes than they are in us being able to see ourselves as unique individuals. Our individual identities are lost in the crowd because that's the goal of branding.

Look at the origin of brands. Brands mark cattle, horses, and other animals to show the world which herd they belong to. Brands were, and still are, used to assign ownership.

Fashion brands do much the same thing. They have recognizable logos and imagery that ultimately stimulate a herd mentality. They use words that effectively corral us into groups with similar desires or attributes: *Sophisticated. Creative. Powerful. Sexy. Outdoorsy. Athletic. Rebellious.*

Fashion branding is highly visible because visibility creates a sense of belonging. We choose specific brands because we want to bask in their images. There is safety associated with being in a community of like-minded individuals. Our brains like that predictability. When people wear clothes or accessories with recognizable images or labels, both the wearers and the observers know which boxes they fit into.

We connect emotionally.

Those of us who work in advertising or marketing know brands are purposely designed to create emotional connections. Brand manufacturers don't want you to be logical about your choices. They want you to identify with and wear their brands because you aspire to the achievements or confidence or youth or beauty or power or strength or whatever their brands stand for. Emotional connection is how brands create loyalty.

Why do you think celebrities are spokespeople and athletes get sponsors? Because their image and success appeals to us, the target audience. We aspire to those same images, which can inspire us to purchase the products or services on offer.

Our aspirations connect us to other people who have similar dreams or who have already achieved our goals. There is a subtle promise that we can achieve the same success—we just need the right image.

Creating the right image has taken on a new dimension with social media as a major source of connection. Branding ourselves has become a big business. Programs, consultants, and frameworks teach us how to stand out and own our space by following their templates and programs.

Not surprisingly, these formulas sometimes contradict each other. Branding experts tell us, "You are your brand." Succession planning experts remind us we need to separate ourselves from our products and services, because we are not *the* brand. And when we have both personal and business or product brands, we're told they need to work in harmony if we want to inspire, excite, and invite others to contribute to our success.

Yes, it can be complex and confusing. We are our own brands, but they aren't us. So how do we avoid becoming emotionally entwined in a brand's success or failure? How do we separate our work, our art, our products, and our services from our human need for acceptance and belonging?

And if we want to be seen and valued as individuals, why are we copying the mass-marketed brands and behaviors of others?

> **SUCCESS IS BELIEVING**
>
> *I can* — *I will* — *I did!*

The answer takes us back to Maslow's Hierarchy. We have a need to be loved. To be accepted. We need to love ourselves and be valued by others in order to feel safe enough to seek fulfillment . . . to become the best we can be. But we must also exercise our power of choice.

We create our own success.

When we believe in ourselves, we don't need to rely on brand labels to show up with confidence. We know we belong to ourselves. We know we have the power to choose what we can do and how we do it.

We succeed by embracing our talents and gifts and believing we not only can succeed, but we also deserve success. When we push past the Expectations Ceiling that threatens to hold us back and embrace uncertainty as an acceptable companion on our journey, we create success on our own terms.

A pause for thought before we leave this chapter:

> **Here's why success is believing:**
>
> We become our thoughts.
> We show up with confidence.
> We connect emotionally.
> We create our own success.

15. SUCCESS IS AN IDENTITY.

Be you. Show, don't tell, by embodying your beliefs. –Stephanie Major

I love words. I talk about them with the same passion other people have when they talk about clothes. To me, there isn't much difference. Both words and clothes influence how we feel about ourselves, and how we show up in the world.

Ask a woman if she has a favorite outfit, and she will probably say she has different favorites for different occasions. Her response indicates how often our clothing choices reflect our desired emotions. We care about what we wear because we want to feel good about ourselves.

The feelings we attach to clothing often determine how we show up. We dress the way we want to be seen, or, in some cases, not seen. We dress to stand out, and we dress to hide.

We care about the clothes we wear.

We may intentionally choose a power color or a stand-out outfit when we're making a key presentation, going on a date, attending an event, or doing something important. Our choice typically reflects the way we want to feel and how we want to be seen by others.

Like many women, I wear a lot of black. It's versatile. Flattering. At one time I would have rationalized wearing black as a practical choice because it blends into almost any occasion. In reality, though, wearing black was me playing small. Staying in the background.

Artist Patricia Gagic changed my perspective. She paints the image of a basic black outfit as the canvas on which we create our presence. Her image captures the essence of identity—a blank canvas presenting us with both boundaries and possibilities. Black becomes the backdrop on which we layer our personality through colors and textures. We can subtly or dramatically touch up, accent, and change our canvas to adapt to the moment.

I now layer my black canvas with bold jewelry and scarves. My choices depend on how I want to express myself. And since I am passionate and emotive, I give myself options. My closet holds dozens of scarves: long and short, square and oblong, patterned and plain. Silks, wools, and prints in shades of red, blue, black and white, and copper each allow me to reflect different sides of who I am.

I also have about a hundred pairs of earrings, which add degrees of subtle professionalism, sensual femininity, stark contrast, stunning color, or simple accents.

By accessorizing with scarves and jewelry, I can carry a dozen different outfits in a packing pouch the size of two hardcover books. Accessories are my secret to traveling with a carry-on suitcase. And my secret for showing up the way I want to be seen.

When I started speaking professionally, I gravitated toward a few specific scarves and earrings. They flatter me, and I feel good when I wear them. I didn't think about why. I didn't analyze my choices. I just enjoyed the confidence they gave me.

It wasn't until someone asked me the story behind a particular scarf, that I realized my preference for certain accessories wasn't about fashion, labels, or color but about my emotional attachment to those items.

Clothes create emotional connection.

Most of us instinctively know this connection. The little black dress that makes us feel sexy. The camel coat that projects a sense of style. The brand-name jeans that tell the world we have good taste. The trainers that imply a dedicated runner. Or the sneakers that express attitude.

Maybe you have certain clothing or colors or brands you associate with confidence. Or curiosity. Or a sense of presence and power. Maybe you have an outfit or a piece of jewelry that brought you luck.

Maybe a particular item makes you look and feel sensual, energetic, or professional.

If you deliberately choose outfits for how you want to show up for a meeting, event, or date, you are on the right track to achieving your goal. There is evidence showing how and why clothing impacts our behavior and choices.

In 2012, researchers at the Kellogg School of Management at Northwestern University demonstrated the connection between our clothing and our mindset.[3] Students were given white lab coats to wear before taking tests that measured cognitive responses. Some of the students were told the lab coats were doctors' coats, and others were told they were painters' coats.

When the results were analyzed, the students who thought they were wearing doctors' coats performed better on the tests than the students wearing what they perceived as painters' coats. Why would it matter which lab coats they were wearing?

The researchers concluded the difference in performance was not about the coats themselves, but rather what the students *thought* about the coats they were wearing. Since a doctor is generally associated with being attentive and careful, the students who believed they were wearing a doctor's lab coat seemed to approach the tests with more sustained attention.

Emotional connection influences how we show up.

The study showed how when we consciously wear things that hold symbolic meanings for us, we tend to behave differently. In other words, when we associate certain emotions or attributes with the clothing we are wearing, our actions and choices reflect the connection we feel. Our thoughts and feelings shape our mindset, which determines our behaviors, and those behaviors affect the outcomes.

The researchers called this effect "enclothed cognition." They postulated that when we put on certain clothes, we're more likely to step into the role the clothing personifies.

Adam Galinsky, one of the leading researchers in enclothed cognition, says it has long been known that "clothing affects how other people perceive us, as well as how we think about ourselves."

If clothes can make a person, what about words? Most of us wear more words than clothes, so what happens when we step into the roles our relationships, titles, or profile descriptions personify? If we substituted *Wordz We Wear* for *clothing* in Galinsky's quote, we'd get: *"The Wordz We Wear affect how other people perceive us, as well as how we think about ourselves."*

Think about it. People are complex. We use dozens, if not hundreds, of words to describe *who* we are. We have specific words to describe our relationships with families, friends, colleagues, and neighbors.

We use other words to talk about our work, professions, careers, and education. Then there are the words we use to talk about our hobbies and passions—the activities and pastimes we love. Often, these are the words that make us smile. They feed the sense of fulfillment we seek.

We also have a set of words to describe our personalities and characteristics. We inherit many of them from our upbringing, we adopt others from the way people talk about us, and we may consciously choose some words for ourselves.

We use all these different words to describe ourselves—but do we think about them? Do we stop to consider the impact of the Wordz We Wear on our mindset, our choices, and our identity?

We need to. The word labels used to describe us actually define us, which means they can also confine us. The words people use to talk about us, as well as the words we use to talk about ourselves, mix with the words our inner voices use to talk to us. All these words influence our beliefs around who we are and what we expect we can and can't do.

The inner voices and the external voices that show up at work, at home, and in relationships can easily manipulate our self-confidence and self-esteem. Since we need that base of confidence and self-worth to be fulfilled, these words are instrumental in our ability to own our identity and choose our future.

As women, we know the impact of brand labels on how we feel about ourselves. We know how wearing specific clothes, shoes, and accessories changes our mood. When we recognize and adapt the power of this emotional connection to our thoughts and words, we have more control over how we *want* to feel and show up.

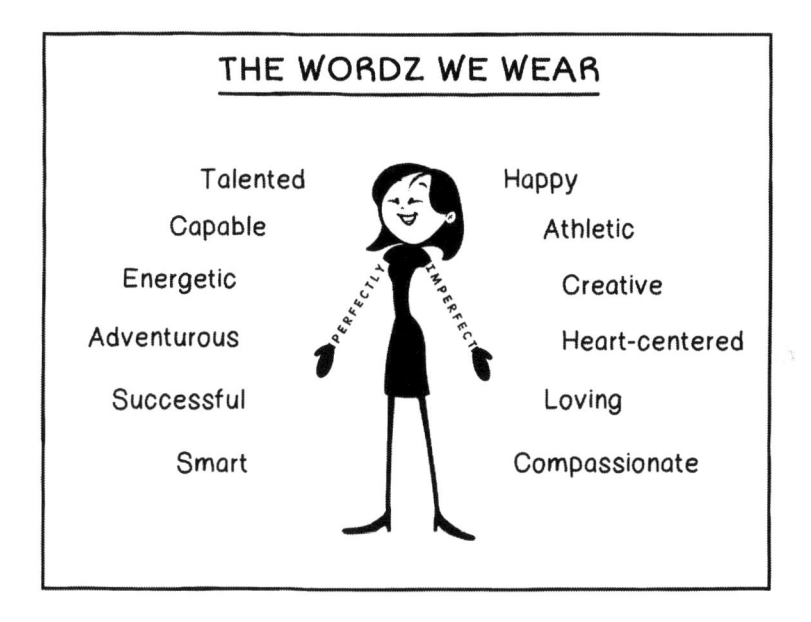

THE WORDZ WE WEAR

Talented
Capable
Energetic
Adventurous
Successful
Smart

Happy
Athletic
Creative
Heart-centered
Loving
Compassionate

PERFECTLY IMPERFECT

Choosing our word labels with intention allows us to step into mindsets conducive to personal growth. Our mindsets influence our actions, behaviors, and choices—the ABCs of identity—so it's easy to see how our choices reflect our sense of identity.

Both clothing and word labels shape our sense of who we are and who we believe we can become. When we emotionally connect to a label, we are adopting the image the label projects. We are either validating how we feel or using the image to help us achieve the feelings we want to have.

The same way we change into jeans or leggings or dresses depending on the occasion, we can change the Wordz We Wear to step into the person we want to be in any situation or role.

The Wordz We Wear reflect our identity.

Words tell us where we fit into society and where and how we don't. They create expectations of what we can and can't do, and what we do or don't deserve.

It bears repeating that if we don't expect to achieve something, we don't pursue it. If we don't pursue it, we will never achieve it. That means if we attach our identity to the wrong words, they limit us. We may never become the person we have the potential to be.

When we intentionally choose wordz that empower us, we start to override the limiting beliefs that restrict our choices—the beliefs that hold us back from discovering our full potential and living our best lives.

The power of wordz is in the images they project. Consciously choosing our wordz can help us intentionally show up with presence. The right wordz allow us to be who we innately are and adopt the mindset of who we want to become.

We don't need to change *who* we are. We need to become *more* of who we are—because we are worth celebrating.

A pause for thought before we leave this chapter:

> **Here's why success is an identity:**
>
> We care about the clothes we wear.
> Clothes create emotional connection.
> Emotional connection influences how we show up.
> The Wordz We Wear reflect our identity.

16. WORDZ OF WISDOM

*Be Loud. Take up Space. Share your voice.
Be true to your Self.* –Alex Cattoni

Writing this book has been one of the scariest and most rewarding experiences of my life. Perhaps the most unexpected gift was the sisterhood I experienced talking with, and listening to, the many women who shared their stories with me. I can't begin to capture everything they taught me, but I want to convey more of their wisdom in this chapter.

Specifically, I want to share their responses to the question: "If you were talking to your daughters, your younger self, or someone you were mentoring, what's one message you'd love these women to know?"

It is impossible to summarize their insight in a paragraph or two. The strength, grace, wisdom, courage, confidence, compassion, and beauty in their responses deserves to be shared in its full glory. And since I can't begin to prioritize these Wordz of Wisdom, they follow in alphabetical order by first name.

Alex Cattoni, founder of the Copy Posse

Be loud. Take up space.

> Share your opinion. Leave a legacy. Change the future for others. Raise the ceiling on possibilities.

Create a life on your terms.

> Women have been taught to be quiet, to be good, to be nice girls, so we are afraid of being our true selves. We go through shy, awkward phases and question ourselves, but success is about getting over the BS and saying what we believe and being who we are.

Take risks.

> It's uncomfortable to put yourself out there but confidence comes through courage. Take risks, prioritize your needs, and find your biggest supporters so you can control and shape your own destiny.

Alex Gabriel, writer

> Listen to your intuition and follow your heart. When you believe in the path you choose, the Universe will support you all the way. You'll make mistakes but your next steps will carry more knowledge. Stay strong and true to your Self.

Alicia Grayeb, sustainability educator and proactive critical thinker

- △ Look after yourself in every way: your health, your priorities, and your needs.
- △ How you speak to yourself matters. Your mind and body are reflections of your thoughts.
- △ All you need is already within you; make sure you nurture yourself with your thoughts and words.
- △ Find a balance between following your heart and making logical decisions. Look for long-term satisfaction, not short-term comfort.
- △ Don't let others dim your light because they think it's too bright. Be bold. Dare to be you.

Anne-Marie Warburton, creator, owner of Gallery Gemma Jewellery

- △ Start developing intuition. Learn to listen. Be honorable.
- △ Believe in yourself. Make your own path . . . there isn't only one way to do things.
- △ Nothing is guaranteed. Stop pushing against what you don't want and start embracing what you do want.

Barbara Ells, proud mom of two

Be confident and proud of who you are.

> Your strengths and talents are not the strengths and talents of others, and you should not compare them. Believing in yourself will help to guide you to your future; travel the path with integrity.

Cathy Sweet, president of Comztar Commercial Properties

You are more powerful than you think.

> Don't doubt yourself so much. Make a decision based on what you know. Some results will turn out better than others, but you've made the decision and you move on from that.

Step into your power.

> Be personally fulfilled and financially independent without your life partner.

Dr. Cheryl Hache Macdonald, chiropractor, mother of two, seeker of truth and love for humanity

> I know you won't always feel loved or love yourself. I know you'll go through challenges. I know you will feel all sorts of feelings you would like someone to take away and make all better.

> However, the gifts you possess need you to figure out how to love yourself. You are unique, but only you have the answers—they are all locked safely inside of you. You will need to push to discover them for yourself.

So please don't get discouraged by your big dreams. You will make them happen one little step at a time. You are so loved!

Darlene Doiron, peace advocate

Be in the flow.

> Life is like a dance where you need to intuitively feel the music of inner dialogue and inner peace; pay attention to that feeling and flow to the sound of it.

Create your playlist.

> Music is composed of high notes and low notes that, when put together, can sound harmonious. The same is true with life. Life has different episodes, and you will need to figure out your own playlist because you are the master of it.

Love is everything: forgive, reset, let go, and let it flow. Happiness is a choice.

Dawn Arnold, mayor of Moncton, New Brunswick, Canada

Just be you. Freedom comes with that. It's a lot easier to just be you than to be what you think everybody thinks you should be.

Edye Hoffmann, founder of Dementia Compass

Live life fully.

> Build as many role models as possible, then make friends with them. Strive to meet people outside your own circle; consider other cultures, genders, and professional or familial

roles. Choose people who are different from yourself, and you'll learn so much about yourself.

Define your self-worth as more than your looks.

Seek what makes you curious, hungry for more, and gets you out of bed in the morning. If you haven't found it yet, keep looking. Your beauty will come from your self-confidence and stay with you for years. Your self-confidence will be what everyone will find so attractive in you.

You may grow into and out of communities where you feel you belong.

That's a good thing. Resilience is built in between communities. This is part of life and will define who you are and what matters to you.

Estelle Doiron, founder and CEO of Koffee Beauty

Have a plan.

Then shoot ten times higher than that plan. Effort is 100 percent associated with the results you get.

Be specific.

The Universe doesn't understand a vague idea. You need to know what you want in order to get what you want.

Focus.

Put your efforts into exactly what you want. If you don't, you're not going to get it.

Fay Milan, Renaissance woman

Listen to yourself.

> Don't let family or friends interfere with your dreams. No one else knows what your soul needs to thrive.

As you move forward in your life, prioritize what you want to achieve.

> Ask yourself what you need to do to touch that goal and give yourself permission to choose how to move forward with or without the support of others. Only you can write your story and reach your shining stars.

Gail Blashyn, seeker of love for humans and animals

- △ Seek adventures, joy, and love with equal passion.
- △ Be brave enough to take risks, to follow a star, and to change course.
- △ Compromise, unless it involves your integrity or the way you deserve to be treated.

Janna Hare, founder and CEO of Spark Leadership Inc.

Listen to your inner leader. Embrace your own extraordinary self-worth. Find delight in the world around you, and don't be afraid to live the life you'd love to write a story about one day.

- △ Attend to your inner ecosystem.
- △ Ask for what you need.
- △ Honor yourself first and foremost.

△ Watch your self-talk because eventually you just might believe it.

△ Regularly be someone else's "believing mirror."

△ Give yourself permission to live an extraordinary life.

Jennifer (JJ) Minella, mindful cybersecurity leader

My advice to my younger self and any young woman is twofold:

1. Always be a leader, even if you're only leading yourself.
2. And never be afraid to be and share your true self; authenticity is the superpower of life, love, and leadership.

Jo Gillibrand, coach, trainer, mindfulness teacher, yoga therapist

Embrace Failure.

> Don't be quite so afraid to fail. It's not so much the failure we worry about as the judgment that goes with it. Don't worry about the judgment that comes with failure. Mistakes have to be experienced. There's no shortcut for learning and growing.

Embrace Confidence.

> I wish I could have been myself at a younger age. Instead of keeping the layers hidden, I wish I'd been more confident to stand in myself.

Forget Perfection.

One of the most disappointing aspects of the growing-up journey is realizing that we're not perfect. But when we're able to accept that disappointment, there's more acceptance in the imperfection. You can relax a bit more. And that's stepping into the Self.

Dr. Julia Sen, the Possibility Psychologist

It's not the Glass Ceiling holding us back. Belonging to ourselves is the key to growth.

Prioritize you.

In order for women to give back, self-care needs to become the new norm for us. We're not wired to care for ourselves, and we need to change that before we collapse. The world is ready. It's time. It's necessary. It's not just a *nice-to-do*. It's the only way to sustain our ability to care and contribute. It's not selfish. We must care for ourselves to be able to give back to others.

Kelsey Reidl, marketing coach, founder of The Visionary Method™, host of the *Visionary Life* podcast

Get in the practice of sharing your thoughts publicly.

> It can be scary, because not all of us are comfortable being visible. We've been told to hide. And sometimes when we did get visible, we were made fun of. But if you want to reach a new level, start to write every day, or record a podcast once a week, or send an email newsletter to friends and family, or make YouTube videos, or get together with a women's circle and express your true desires.

Find your voice.

> Engage in some sort of practice where you feel like you're finding your voice and potentially figuring out who you are. We learn a lot about ourselves when we put words behind our feelings. Self-expression helps us to grow and to evolve by exploring our thoughts and seeing what comes up.

Lynn Byrgesen, enriched wife, mother, individual

> You are the architect of your life experiences. Do not be a spectator. Articulate, embark on, and implement your personal and professional goals.
>
> Acknowledge your strengths and passions by compiling a *to-be* list. Motivate, challenge, and empower yourself. Seek and advocate for a mentor(s). Accept feedback.
>
> Take risks to learn your tolerance and resiliency levels. Challenge your fears. Plan for the expected and the unexpected.
>
> Be inquisitive. Read to enrich your vocabulary, enhance your conversational abilities, and expand your fields of knowledge.
>
> Respect different points of view, effort over ability, and integrity over ego. Talk less and actively listen more.
>
> Live for the moments you can't put into words. Be adventurous. Invest in yourself. Laugh. Love. And strive to be all you are.

Lori Olson, software app developer and trainer, founder of 6 Pack Apps

Understand what your skills are, and what you're good at, and then don't let anybody tell you you're not good. Pursue whatever you need to do to learn and excel at the things you want to do.

If the people around you don't appreciate you, keep looking for people like you, who will support you. It's easier than ever to find your tribe.

Melissa Duguay, international platform artist

Find your own definition of balance.

> It's different for everyone, but make sure that every aspect of your life is fulfilled—mind, body, and soul.

Don't worry about mistakes.

> You don't grow if you don't fail. Success is a work in progress.

Mischka Jacobs, *Say YES to yourself*

Say YES to yourself.

- △ Put money into your YES Fund so you can say yes to doing whatever you want with courage and grace.
- △ Yes, I can quit my job and live in New York for a year to learn five languages.
- △ Yes, I can step out on my own and try entrepreneurship.
- △ Yes, I can do this for fun, not for a house or for retirement.

Say YES to life.

△ Live a rich and bold life filled with experience and stories you'll tell the grandkids. The Good, the Bad, the Ugly, the Funny, the Beautiful . . . all of it.

△ Ask yourself: *At the end of the day, did I live enough? Did I live boldly enough? Did I make choices that scared me, but I made them anyway? Did I bet on myself? Did I bet on others? Did I help them?*

Say YES to others.

△ If you really truly want to help women, give them the work. Don't just talk about it. Give women the work.

Natacha Dugas, founder of RavingFan.io

Go for it. Be obsessed!

> I would tell myself or anyone to be obsessed with what you want to achieve. When any other thoughts, anxiety, or doubts come to mind, set them aside and focus on what you want to achieve and why you want to achieve it. Do not be distracted by useless thinking that doesn't serve the achievement of your goals.
>
> I am obsessed with three things: my family, my business, and myself. I push aside any thoughts that don't serve the achievement of these goals.

Nicol Drayton, woman on a journey to Self

1. Stop comparing yourself to others.
2. No one is better than you.
3. Go for what you want, no matter how impossible or how unreachable it seems.

Patricia K. Gagic, contemporary artist, author, activist, humanitarian

We all can't have the same gifts. We all can't be the same. But we can learn from one another. What do I see in you I like? What do you see in me? How can we guide and help each other grow and develop?

What knowledge can you unravel enough that somebody else will appreciate it? How can you provide your knowledge and gifts in a way someone else can receive and benefit from them?

Polish the stones they are stepping on and help them to get to the next one.

Renée Warren, founder and CEO of We Wild Women

Consistency is your currency.

> Decide how often and with how much intensity you're willing to show up to grow your business, or to be a parent, and then be proud of that decision. You can adjust as you go, but don't cave into the need to work sixty hours a week.

Believe in yourself.

Who cares what that college professor said to you? Who cares what your grade three teacher said? You're an adult. You can make your own decisions. You can find your own solutions. Ask for help. Then go through it.

Go through it.

When we face moments of adversity and conflict, whether internal or external, sometimes the fastest way is to just go through it. The only way to heal a trauma is to face the trauma, whether it's a big one or a little one. The more you keep avoiding it, the longer it's going to live in your life. I wish I'd have known this a long time ago.

Sally Ng, CEO, community builder, board member, facilitator, world traveler, dog lover

Think. Don't be afraid to try things out.

We get so comfortable in our everyday world that we're scared to change jobs. We're scared to go on dates. By not trying things, we close ourselves in a corner.

Stop floundering; make a decision.

Ask yourself, *What's the worst thing that's going to happen?* The only two things I think about are: *Is it legal?* and *Will I have some fun? If not, why not?*

Sharon Preszler, keynote speaker, transition coach, fighter pilot

You get to decide who gets inside your head because you get to decide who matters to you.

You get to decide whose opinion matters. There will always be people telling you what you should do, what you're not good at, that you're not good enough, blah, blah, blah. You get to decide who you listen to.

If you take people's opinions on the same level as how you value them, you're going to be able to do what you want because you are going to be focused on the people who are supportive of you. And no matter what your goal is, as long as you work toward it—even if you don't reach it—you've done better than just sitting on your couch and not trying.

You've got to try. Don't try to be the best so that people will say, "Oh, you're amazing." Try to be your best because you want to be the best.

Shirlee Sharkey, former president and CEO of SE Health, board director and adviser, president of SS Consulting strategic leadership and health care advisory services

Think things through if you want to have an impact. If you don't design it, it will not happen.

Don't ever stay at a place where you need it more than it needs you. You need to be bold and make change happen, but do not fool yourself in the process.

Take your work incredibly seriously, but don't take yourself too seriously for more than five seconds. Why? Because two hundred years from now, you are completely irrelevant.

Stephanie Major, intentional life creator, host of *The Major Magic Show* podcast

No language can highlight how important or how fulfilling it is to be yourself. Telling my girls something is one thing, but until I step out and do what I'm saying, I'm not showing them that it's okay for them to do what they believe in.

I have to *be* it. I have to courageously *do* it. By living my life that way, I let my girls know that they can take the same steps for themselves. They can get a taste of being boldly themselves.

Living intentionally is a practice. It's not perfect, and there are definitely moments where I lose myself a little, but when I feel that vibration, that resonance, that power and freedom, it creates momentum. Then I know the reason I'm taking a big step is because I'm strong enough to take it.

Stephanie Winger, maven entrepreneur

If I could time travel back a few decades, I would whisper words of encouragement like:

"You've got this."

"You deserve this."

"It'll be so much better than you can imagine."

Tammy Price, Shifting into High Gear

Surrender to who you are so that you can lead the next generation.

Surrender is what opens us up to expansion. Surrender is where our intuitive capabilities come in. Surrender is when we are able to get to the place where we feel excited about the inevitable adventures that are going to unfold over which we have no control.

That point when we get into the space where it's exciting versus uncomfortable? That's activating feeling in the body and leaning into surrender.

Veronica Piacek, marketing guru, consultant, entrepreneur

Own what you've been given.

Put your stamp on it. Women worry too much about saying no or setting boundaries or making life decisions.

Don't be scared to learn as much as you can. Step up, ask for advice, get seen and heard.

Perfection is procrastination.

We have such a need to be prepared that sometimes we don't take the next step. Planning is important, but so is action, so work with others to create progress.

A pause for thought before we leave this chapter:

> ## Future YOU is you with intention:
>
> Show up with confidence. You matter.
> Your story matters. Your desires matter.
> Your gifts matter. Your fears matter.
> Your voice matters. Your worries matter.
> Your love matters. Your wordz matter.
>
> ....
>
> Believe in yourself.
> You are more than enough.
> Believe in possibilities.
> Own your future.

THE LAST WORDZ

> Like confidence, success is a practice.
> —Estelle Doiron

Permission to be yourself.

I don't usually cry in public.

But this day was different. I walked into the changing room as my husband was wrapping up a post-game review of the hockey game with the team he coached.

I don't know if you've ever been in a hockey change room, but the first thing that hits you is the stench. Sweat, mildew, urine, ripe bananas, oranges, excitement, disappointment . . . there's an all-out assault on the senses when you walk into the changing room at an ice arena.

But it wasn't the smell or the noise that made me cry that day.

It was my eight-year-old daughter, Danai. She was sitting beside her dad—her coach—drinking from a water bottle and swinging her legs. I motioned that it was time to go or we'd be late for her next activity. Our feisty little defense player jumped up, whipped off her hockey jersey, and transformed.

She was wearing a pink bodysuit and a fluffy white tutu under her bulky hockey clothes. We were going from hockey to ballet.

Danai was never taught that girls were too "fragile" to play hockey. She didn't know some people thought girls couldn't and shouldn't be fast and aggressive on the ice. She was blissfully unaware that there were supposedly limits to the type of sports she could participate in as a girl.

My daughter didn't have to choose between being feminine or being strong. Or being graceful versus forceful. She had never been told she couldn't be both. Neither she nor her brother were exposed to language that said they had to conform to traditional roles.

As working parents who frequently traveled on business, Marcel and I sometimes struggled with our choices. We wanted to raise our kids to accept their strengths and make their own decisions, yet neither of us had role models to turn to. We constantly danced a jig with doubt and determination.

But that day, as I watched my little girl whip off her smelly hockey jersey and turn into a lithe dancer, I knew we had done okay. Our daughter's world was ripe with opportunities. She innately sensed she could do whatever she wanted to do.

Hell, yes, I cried.

Danai just shook her head, punched Dad-Coach in the arm, and grabbed her hockey bag—a bag almost as big as she was.

Because she could.

WORDZ OF GRATITUDE

Thank you doesn't begin to capture the gratitude I have for all you women who shared your time and trauma, doubts and dreams with me. I learned so much as we delved into your stories, struggles, loves, values, fears, pain, abandonment, depression, and resilience. Your candor and grace changed my life and will certainly impact the lives of countless others. I am honored that you gave me permission to share your names, stories, and Wordz of Wisdom. You are role models, mentors, muses, and tangible evidence that women can change the world for the better. Thank you for being in my life and sharing your amazingness.

To my friend Janna Hare: I'm glad you broke a toe all those years ago and transitioned from my husband's coach to a dear friend. Your questions, your formal and informal coaching, and your *Dare to Lead* workshop inspired me to address my limiting beliefs by writing a novel. That novel . . . and all the conversations we had around fear, identity, and worthiness . . . got me curious about why we place limits and ceilings on ourselves and ultimately led to this book. Thank you for all those meandering conversations.

To the women who attended Janna's *Dare to Lead* workshop with me: I don't think I ever thanked you for helping me find the confidence to express myself. By reading my novel, *A Rose Is Just a Rose,* and showing up for a book-club–style discussion, you helped me let go of my past and embrace my gifts. While the novel wasn't published, completing it liberated me in ways I never imagined possible. Thank you for caring and crying with me.

To Natacha Dugas, my #1 Raving fan: You never stop. From the moment we connected, you encouraged me to step into my voice. You nudged, nourished, and nagged (in a nice way). Plus, you unselfishly shared your skills and knowledge to help me navigate social media, websites, funnels, and acronyms. Merci beaucoup, ma chère.

To the many other women who encouraged me, pushed me, and read drafts . . . to those who gave me feedback, pep talks, insight and even the occasional kick in the butt: I love you. I value your honesty, your unwavering support, and your friendship. Alex, Barb, Edye, Lori, Michelle, Jo, Julia, Patricia, Tammy, Major, Stephanie, Anne-Marie, Theano, Jennifer, Stefanie, Leisa, Julie . . . and many other incredible women who showed up to keep me motivated. You kept me going when

I started to doubt myself. Thank you. You made this book possible.

To Jen Singer, "Machete Jen." I love you and hate you. Your initial feedback on this book sent me back to why I was writing it, and I cut 80 percent of the content I'd already written. It was one of the hardest things I have ever done and one of the best things I have ever done. (I guess I earned my own machete.) This book is so much better for you. No words can capture my appreciation for you and your art.

To Amy Port and Michael Port of Heroic Public Speaking (HPS). First, thank you for introducing me to Jen Singer! Second, the storytelling tricks you taught us for speaking changed the way I approached stories in my book. *Yes, and . . .* that gave them more purpose and power. Thank you for inspiring me to share my story with more people.

To my dear HPS Alumni cohorts. What can I say? You blow me away with your passion, confidence, commitment, and energy. I feel alive in your auras. You inspired and supported me as I expanded the theory of the Wordz We Wear into a keynote and workshop. I am honored and grateful to know you.

To the team at Soul Seed: Thank you for welcoming me as an author and helping me bring this book to life. Being supported by a team of talented and dedicated women is one of the most rewarding aspects of publishing my book. *The Wordz We Wear* wouldn't be the same without your care and attention.

To my late parents, Helen and Lawrence Milan. Dad, you taught me about love and forgiveness. I am grateful for your patience in teaching me. Mom, you taught me it was never too late to pursue our dreams and your years with Alzheimer's also unintentionally showed me we never know when we might lose our ability to communicate . . . so I had better stop procrastinating and start doing. Thank you for these life lessons.

To my youngest sister—my soul sister and best friend—Gail Blashyn: You have been with me through this journey longer than anyone else. I don't think I could have done it without you. Not only do you laugh out loud with me, but you also cry with me and love me unconditionally. You challenge me, cheer me up, give me honest feedback, and won't accept excuses. I trust you and love you beyond the constraints of time. Massive hugs, Gailo!

To Lynn, Iris, Fay, Hope, Cherry, and Loretta: Sisters, in your own ways, you all contributed to pushing me to finish this book. Some of you weren't surprised I'd write a book, some of you listened compassionately as I fought with writer's block, and some of you questioned why I was taking on a new challenge at this stage of my life. I found clarity and conviction through all these interactions. Thank you.

To Kyle and Danai: The two of you add dimension to my identity. Being your mother is one of the greatest joys in my life. You constantly teach me how expansive love is, and you've helped me explore how we become better versions of ourselves by accepting who we are. I am immeasurably proud of you both, and I'm excited to see where your life choices and dreams take you.

And to Marcel: When you entered my life, you changed my world. You helped me understand I was no longer defective. You taught me what it felt like to be loved without limits. You made me see that underneath all the scars, there was a little girl who just wanted to express joy. You encouraged that little girl. You danced with her. You created a family with her. You traveled the world with her. You built a business with her. Most importantly, you believed in her when she set off on this soul mission to write a book. I love you beyond words.

And to *little Vera*: You did it. You found your voice. Thank you for patiently waiting until I was ready to listen.

END NOTES

[1] https://www.simplypsychology.org/self-fulfilling-prophecy.html

[2] https://www.simplypsychology.org/maslow.html

[3] https://www.sciencedirect.com/science/article/abs/pii/S0022103112000200

THE WORDZ WE WEAR BOOK CLUB PROMPTS

1. The author suggests you can read the book chapter by chapter or skip to the sections that interest you. Which did you do and why?

2. The author links showing up with confidence to both the clothes we wear and the way we talk to and about ourselves. What clothes or accessories do you wear that boost your confidence?

3. How much do you relate to the idea that word labels, like clothing labels, affect how you feel and how you show up in the world?

4. What wordz do you, or could you, use to introduce yourself that might help you feel more confident?

5. What parts of the book either challenge or reinforce your ideas or beliefs regarding what's holding you back from living your best life?

6. The author shared anecdotes from other women to support her theories. Which women or their stories do you relate to?

7. The book explores the various ceilings that can prevent us from creating our best life. Can you identify how any of them affect you?

8. Why does the author spell wordz with a "z" rather than an "s"?

9. The chapter on Wordz of Wisdom contains advice from dozens of women. Does any of their advice surprise you? Which suggestions inspire you the most?

If you or your book club would like to explore the concepts outlined in *The Wordz We Wear* in more depth, visit https://www.veragervais.com/wordz-resources and download The Wordz We Wear Discussion Guide

AUTHOR BIO

VERA MILAN GERVAIS is a speaker, author, award-winning businesswoman, and mindset mentor who helps women develop confidence in themselves and their leadership skills. Her signature Wordz We Wear® program inspires women to challenge limiting labels and create their best life.

Vera knows firsthand that the way we describe ourselves can directly impact the way we show up. A birth defect that resulted in four major surgeries before she turned eighteen left her with a leg length difference, scoliosis, and osteoarthritis. Managing her health while building careers as an entrepreneur, professional writer, marketer, and strategic consultant influenced Vera's perspective on balancing success and well-being.

An adventurous introvert, Vera is an avid hiker, gardener, and photographer who has climbed mountains, come face-to-face with a python, built several businesses with her husband, and explored all seven continents with her family!

The mother of two talented and amazing young adults, Vera lives near the ocean in New Brunswick, Canada, with her husband and business partner Marcel and a hundred pairs of earrings.

https://www.veragervais.com/
https://www.linkedin.com/in/vera-milan-gervais/
https://www.facebook.com/vera.milan.gervais
https://www.amazon.ca/Vera-Milan-Gervais/e/B0C444ZGJP/ref

SOUL SEED
LEGACY·HOUSE

At Soul Seed Legacy House, we help thought leaders and creative entrepreneurs capture their vision in the form of nonfiction books, journals, workbooks, affirmation cards, and personal growth products.

Our mission is to help our authors grow and scale a platform far beyond the book, protect their soul's work, and turn their message into a legacy!

www.sslegacyhouse.com

@sslegacyhouse

Manufactured by Amazon.ca
Bolton, ON